To Professor Rich[illegible]

with kind regards

from the translator

[illegible]

The University of Chicago

May 22, 2014

ZENON ROZANSKI
Mützen ab
NE REPORTAGE AUS DER STRAFKOMPANIE DES KZ. AUSCHWITZ

Caps Off . . .

A Report about the Punishment Company (SK) of the KZ Auschwitz

BY ZENON ROZANSKI

Translated by
Christine C. Schnusenberg

WITH A FOREWORD BY HERMANN LANGBEIN

RESOURCE *Publications* · Eugene, Oregon

CAPS OFF . . .
A Report about the Punishment Company (SK) of the KZ Auschwitz

Resource Publications
An Imprint of Wipf and Stock Publishers
199 W. 8th Ave., Suite 3
Eugene, OR 97401
www.wipfandstock.com

ISBN 13: 978-1-62032-619-0
Manufactured in the U.S.A.

FRITZ KÜSTER SERIES–ARCHIVE

Edited by Stefan Appelius und Gerhard Kraiker

The Fritz Küster Series–Archive for History and Literature of the Peace Movement at the University of Oldenburg was founded in April 1987. The archive was structured around the estate of the former president of the "German Society for Peace," Fritz Küster (1889–1966), who, during the 1920s and after 1945, effectively held an outstanding position in the German Peace Movement. Küster was the editor of the Pacifist Weekly, *Das andere Deutschland* (The other Germany). During the dictatorship of National Socialism, he was incarcerated in concentration camps for political reasons for more than five years.

In the meantime, the Fritz Küster Series–Archive contains more than twenty estates and fragments of estates of important personalities of the German-speaking Peace Movement; they are concentrated mainly around the time after 1945. The holdings of Dr. Gerhard Gleissberg, Dr. Theodor Michaltscheff, and Dr. Stefan Matzenberger deserve special attention here. Stefan Appelius is responsible for the organization of the archive. The scholarly direction and the consultation of the archive are in the hands of:

Prof. Dr. Gerhard Kraiker (Political Science)
Prof. Dr. Werner Boldt (History)
Prof. Dr. Dirk Grathoff (Literature)

Address:
Fritz Küster–Archiv
Universität Oldenburg
Postfach 25 03D–2900 Oldenburg
Germany

In Memory of Zenon Rozanski and
the Countless Victims of Auschwitz

Contents

Translator's Remarks

I AM DEDICATING MY English translation of *Mützen ab . . .* to its author, Zenon Rozanski. This Report, describing his experiences of the horrors of the Punishment Company (SK) of the KZ Auschwitz, emerges as the voice of the innumerable unrecorded victims of the diabolically organized atrocities in the death chambers of National Socialism. This narrative, however, also gives testimony to an undaunted human spirit that was able to endure und overcome the most inhumane and heinous conditions of the infamous enterprise of National Socialism. Because of his survival in the hell of the KZ Auschwitz, this individual voice of Zenon Rozanski should be heard by the members of the international community. Among the immense volumes of the publications and translations of the works about Nazi—and SS—concentration and death camps, Zenon Rozanski's Report and its translation into English merit a worthy place in the context of the search for the historical truth about the dominance of National Socialism in Germany. With his talent—and perhaps his calling—as a journalist, the prisoner Rozanski was able to observe and document the darkness of the most gruesome details, yet he was also able to get a glimpse of some miraculous glimmers of light and love—in the hellish conditions of Auschwitz. Thus, he has preserved them for all times to come.

I would like to thank Wipf and Stock for their willingness to publish this translation of Rozanski's Report—which is long overdue—thus making it available to the wider English-speaking world. I wish to acknowledge the valuable fascilitating help of Christian Amondson. The free-lance copyeditor, Rochelle Zappia, deserves my appreciation for her good work.

The competent staff of the ITServices of the University of Chicago Regenstein Library deserve my special gratitude because they efficiently assisted me in the navigation of the ever changing Internet cosmos.

Special recognition and gratitude are due to the initiative of the guardians of the Fritz Küster Series–Archive of the University of Oldenburg for having preserved and republished this Report by Zenon Rozanski. I am humbly grateful to Professor Dr. Gerhard Kraiker for permitting me to translate this work into English and for transferring the copyright to me. I also wish to commend Frau Barbara Sip of the bis–Verlag of the University of Oldenburg for her efficiency, kindness, and helpfulness in facilitating the various aspects of this translation project.

In addition to the work itself by Rozanski, the introductions by Professor Dr. Hermann Langbein and Dr. med. Winfried Oster are very important contributions because they provide additional information about the unfathomable creation of the KZ Auschwitz and the incomprehensible actions of extermination by the SS in that death camp with the introduction of poisonous gas Zyklon B. Through their portrait of this dauntless and imaginative Polish journalist and KZ prisoner, Zenon Rozanski, and with their reference to and praise of his invaluable contribution of *Mützen ab . . .* for posterity, Professor Langbein and Dr. Oster have supplied a broader context and background in which to search for the historical truth in the grim reality of National Socialism. They have also given a most valuable description of the situation and mood prevailing in post-war Germany regarding the initial repression of the reality of the existence of concentration and death camps in Germany, and the gradual acceptance and courage to confront these horrible historical facts, after the Auschwitz Trial in Frankfurt from 1963 to 1965.

The translation itself was a daunting task for me. It was emotionally exhausting because I found myself exposed to the gates of hell, a world of incomprehensible, diabolic bestiality in the death chambers of the KZ Auschwitz. In addition, it was often very difficult, if not impossible, to render the Nazi-SS terminology in a somewhat intelligible, fluent, idiomatic English. This difficulty arose mainly from the fact that in addition to its idiosyncrasies, the Nazi-SS terminology was a "coded language"[1] intended to mislead and obfuscate its real meaning and purpose. For instance, in Germany the "code word" *Sonderaktion* was generally understood as a common special treatment for special groups; for the SS in Poland and in Auschwitz, however, it masked the act of execution, especially of Jews. In the translation of regular German, the code term *Sonderbehandlung* could mean "special treatment"; in Auschwitz it was the "legal code word" for

1. Kogon, *Nazi Mass Murder*, 1, 5-12. 159-161; see also, "Euthanasia," 13-51.

"extermination and gassing." The Nazi-SS term *Sonderkommando* would mean "special work detachment" in the translation of regular German, but in Auschwitz it referred to groups of Jewish prisoners who were required to unload the murdered corpses from the gas chambers. The regular translation of *Kapo* or *Vorarbeiter* would be "foreman" or "overseer." But in Auschwitz they were the most brutal henchmen and murderers. Therefore, I have tried to give, after the first citation, an approximate English equivalent for most of the specialized Nazi-SS and KZ terminology. After that I have retained the German expressions throughout the text of the translation in order to maintain unambiguously the SS-KZ context. However, at the end I have provided glossary appendices listing the most common Nazi-SS terms and their approximate English equivalents.

I have retained Rozanski's temporal expressions, most of which are in the present tense. This use gives his narrative an immediacy which the author must still have experienced while he was writing down his Report *Mützen ab. . . .* I have also retained the ellipses which he used after many sentences; these indicate a situation still in progress—either of fear and desperation or of anticipation and hope. He was liberated in 1945; his foreword at the completion of *Mützen ab. . .* is dated 1947. (This explains the immediacy of his recollections.) The first publication followed in 1948. I also have retained the original format of his Report in order to avoid distorting its author's voice and frame of mind. I will also preserve the imprint of the Fritz Küster Series–Archive of the University of Oldenburg because of its important role in Germany during National Socialism and the postwar years. They deserve our gratitude for securing and publishing the work of Zenon Rozanski, *Mützen ab . . . Eine Reportage aus der Strafkompanie des KZ Auschwitz.* That work is now before us in English translation as: *Caps off . . . A Report from the Punishment Company (SK) of the KZ Auschwitz,* published by Wipf and Stock.

Christine C. Schnusenberg, PhD
Translator
University of Chicago
August, 2012

Foreword

THROUGHOUT THE ENTIRE WORLD, Auschwitz has become known as the camp where bureaucratic, alarmingly and perfectly organized mass extermination of human beings found its abysmal culmination when the most modern means available at that time was applied: poison gas Zyklon B (hydrogen cyanide). For this reason, Auschwitz has become the symbol of the realization of the murderous ideology of National Socialism.

Less known, however, is the fact that the concentration camp Auschwitz had already existed since June 14, 1940 and that in its first epoch it was relatively small and detained primarily members of the Polish intelligentsia. Since spring 1942, however, people such as Jews, and later also Gypsies, were deported to Auschwitz only because they were "guilty"—in the eyes of the National Socialist Regime—of belonging to a "race" whose right to life that regime had denied: Once in Auschwitz, they were subjected to those infamous selections during which it was decided which of these deportees were to be marked as "fit for work" and therefore could be admitted as prisoners to the stock of the camp. This decision placed the prisoners in the armament industry where they were made available as a "human shield for production." Those who were considered "unfit for work" were immediately murdered in one of the gas chambers.

Reports about these selections and about life in the shadows of the oversized crematories with their installed gas chambers have been translated into many languages. Courts had to deal with the mass murders for which the judicial system had no precedents available to impart justice in such a scope. For this reason, Auschwitz became a synonym for those crimes which differentiated National Socialism from all other Fascist regimes.

Less known is the first period of Auschwitz during which time this KZ was different from many others. It was different mainly because Poles had to live and die there. Reports written by Poles who had survived this period were rarely translated into other languages. Those who equate Auschwitz with the Holocaust, "the Final Solution of the Jewish Question," as the Holocaust was called in bureaucratic German National Socialism, can overlook the fact that for many Poles Auschwitz remained in their collective memory a place of martyrdom for their nation.

The Pole Zenon Rozanski had to experience this first epoch in the history of Auschwitz. He was able to survive. After the liberation, he had the strength to describe this experience without any national blinkers. The SS sentenced him to a term of fifteen months in the Punishment Company (SK). Afterwards, he remained in Auschwitz and began to write in German a Report about the Punishment Company (SK) of the KZ Auschwitz, which he titled *Mützen ab . . .* In 1948, when this small book appeared, Auschwitz was a taboo topic in Germany. The edition may also have been limited perhaps because of paper scarcity, and therefore, Rozanski's Report remained to a large extent unknown.

This situation might be regarded as characteristic of that time, when this subject was generally avoided because it would have confronted a generation with the question of what they had known at that time, what they had suspected, and how they themselves had acted. And it should not be considered atypical for the present time that, in contrast to the generation before them, the younger generation of Germans has now recognized the significance of this subject matter. One person of this generation has taken pains to make possible the new edition of Rozanski's Report.

He deserves our gratitude for enabling future generations to learn about what was possible in the Punishment Company (SK) of Auschwitz, which was under the direction of the SS. "I limit myself, while writing down these facts"—that is, those happenings which he had to experience in the Punishment Company (SK)—"to a true photographic representation of a reality which still a short while ago determined my daily life," wrote Rozanski in his introduction. Towards the end of his Report, he describes what Symek Rosenthal—a Jew from Cichenau—told him. In the summer of 1942, when the extermination machinery had already been constructed, Rosenthal had to "work" near one of the gas chambers. The *Sonderkommando* (special detachment) to which he was assigned had to haul out from a "room" the gassed corpses. At one time, it was the corpse of Rosenthal's father.

The first period of Auschwitz passed into the next—the one which was to be designated as the "Final Solution." Rosenthal cannot report to anyone. Rozanski has done it for him. He has experienced and survived Auschwitz. It is good that *Mützen ab . . .* is again available for reading.

Hermann Langbein
Vienna, June 1991

Introduction

AUSCHWITZ: EXTERMINATION CAMP. RAMP. Selection. Zyklon B.

Auschwitz was, however, also a Labor Camp. Hunger, anguish, threats, fear, death were awaiting those who seemed fit for work to the examining physician either in the camp or on the ramp. From the beginning, it was planned to exterminate the Jews by way of labor. It was, however, intended to utilize their energy reserves for the SS State; about three to four months were anticipated as the time frame of their work. In 1942, the maximal life span of the Jews in Auschwitz amounted to six months. Jews were already being transported to Auschwitz in 1941. However, Auschwitz was originally designated as a Concentration Camp (KZ) for Polish resistance fighters, intellectuals, and other Poles who appeared to be dangerous to the National Socialist regime. A former Austrian army barrack existed in a sparsely populated area south of Kattowitz with favorable connections to the Polish railroad network which had intermittently been utilized by the German Army.

The SS considered this location an excellent one. Therefore, in August 1941, in Berlin, Himmler gave his infamous order to the first KZ commander, Rudolf Hoess, to expand the Camp of Auschwitz for the extermination of European Jews. At the Wannsee Conference of January 20, 1942, the logistics for the extermination were clarified.

In addition to Auschwitz, there were five other large extermination camps. They were built between 1941 and 1942 and began operating around the middle of 1942. These were the camps of Belzec, Sobibor, Treblinka, Lublin (Majdanek), and Kulmhof (Chelmo). Even today, they can be found on maps because they bear the names of the cities which were located in their vicinity.

When the first camp, which was later called Base Camp Auschwitz I, was no longer sufficient, the Camp Birkenau (Auschwitz II) was built. It was three kilometers away from Auschwitz I. This part began operating in 1942, and in 1943 it was made the largest extermination center of all times. Here, more than 1,000,000 Jews were murdered.

The Camp of Birkenau for women prisoners consisted almost entirely of so-called horse stable barracks. In that place, the conditions were like the ones that Zenon Rozanski described for Block 7 of the camp for men at Birkenau.

From his position as a prisoner in the Punishment Company (SK), Zenon Rozanski was never able to obtain a comprehensive overview of the conditions in the KZ Auschwitz. Therefore, we strongly recommend that our readers also read the books by the Secretary of the Comité Internationale des Camps, Hermann Langbein. The titles are listed in the Appendix.

The colors in the left-hand corners of their chests made it possible to determine to which particular group the prisoners belonged. Through these colors, as well as the numbers which were tattooed into the skin of the left forearms and later fixed unto the clothes, the prisoners—in the eyes of the SS—ceased to exist as persons. The green ones, the *BVs* (*Befristete Vorbeugungshäftlinge),* were officially "restricted prisoners in preventive custody"; unofficially, they were habitual criminals. These were most often the worst prisoners and were frequently as brutal as the SS. However, even among those, there were exceptions. The red corner, on the other hand, designated political prisoners, thus, also Zenon Rozanski, the journalist from Warsaw. Many BVs (green ones) rendered great service to their comrades. Eugen Kogon describes in his book *Der SS-Staat* the fights between the red and green ones for predominance in the camps. The fate of thousands of individuals sometimes depended on who would be the winner.

I read Rozanski's report, as it is now before us, for the first time as a young man during the 1950s. My interest in the debate about the crimes of the NS regime was sparked by discussions in the home of my parents.

Later, I tried to research the biography of Rozanski after the collapse of the National Socialist regime. However, it was already too late. His traces are lost in Brazil. My research, which I conducted with the help of many authorities and individuals, came to an end in the 1970s. The present book is the only one which Rozanski wrote. It was published for the first time in 1948 by the Fritz Küster Verlag in Hannover. Although it was printed on paper of poor quality, it appeared in a relatively high edition. Its reception was probably minimal during the bad times of the post-war years. That was certainly the case during the better times at the beginning of the *Wirtschaftswunder* (economic miracle), when the SS-State was a matter of only the recent past. At that time, the repression of the earlier period was achieved almost to perfection. It was not until the Auschwitz Trial in Frankfurt during the years of 1963 through 1965 that there was a growing awareness of the crimes in the German concentration camps and, consequently, an increased readiness to confront these facts.

Today, as at that time, we hear the opinion expressed that the past events should finally be put to rest. The growing of the extreme right in the German Federal Republic must be stemmed. However, the repression has to be balanced against the reports, books and lectures of former KZ prisoners so that the truth can time and again pave the way. The new edition of the work *Mützen ab . . .*, published by the Fritz Küster–Archiv of the University of Oldenburg ought to be perceived in this sense. I wish this book a wide circulation, especially among young readers.

Dr. Med. Winfried Oster
Herdecke

Preface

This book has nothing in common with the so-called literature. It is a collection of true events that took place during my stay in the Punishment Company (SK) of the Concentration Camp Auschwitz. A few witnesses to these events have also survived the Camp and are now providing the "proof of truth." All names mentioned in this book are real.

I limit myself, in writing down these facts, to a truthful, photographic reproduction of a reality which until recently constituted my daily life.

In order to make my work easier, I have selected from the immense fullness of the multifarious events those which placed me personally closer to the reality of the life in the Camp. My experiences are, however, not unusual. If every former prisoner of a Concentration Camp would write down his personal memoirs, they all would have in common the same sense despite the variety of events they experienced because every prisoner would have felt in a similar way the spirit of the Concentration Camp.

I dedicate this book to the "old guard" of Auschwitz whose bloodily earned experience and comradely sacrifice saved quite a few comrades who arrived later. I dedicate it to those who were still able to experience freedom and to those who fell in front of the Black Wall of the Execution Block, Number 11.

Hannover, 1947
The Author

Zenon Rozanski, a journalist, was born on 10.01.1904 in Warsaw. Rozanski was imprisoned in the KZ Auschwitz from 1941 to 1944. At the end, he was camp senior in the adjacent camp of Buchenwald, Eschershausen-Holzen, near Holzminden. Rozanski lived after the collapse of the NS dictatorship in Hannover, and in 1948 he emigrated to Brazil.

1

"Prisoner 8214 is obediently reporting to the *Strafrapport (Penal Registry)* . . ." *SS-Hauptsturmführer* (Captain), Fritzsch, the *Lagerführer* (camp leader) of the KZ Auschwitz, was sitting behind a wide desk beneath a picture of the Führer. He raised his head . . .

"Well . . ." Small, black, goggle eyes were scrutinizing my erect posture. "What mischief have you been up to?"

"I have taken two dishes of garbage from the SS kitchen," I shouted as loudly as I could.

Fritzsch's eyes flared up . . .

"What? You have taken? You have stolen, you, you dog! The garbage from the kitchen is designated for the fattening of the pigs, and the pigs are for the SS . . . Sabotage!!!" For a moment, he broke off, and then: "Have you already been punished??"

"No."

He looked at me inquisitively.

"How long have you been in the camp?"

"A half year."

SS–Hauptsturmführer Fritzsch stood up. Slowly he swayed on his comically thin X-legs toward me. The pale yellow face of the liver patient began to crimson . . .

"A half year," he repeated. "Since when have you been stealing from the German state?"

"This was the first time," I began, but a well-aimed punch in the stomach prevented me from finishing the sentence.

"Shut up, you are lying! If you had not been stealing, you would have already been flying through the chimney during the last three months; that has been calculated scientifically." Briefly he looked at me. "You are living too long." He turned to the prisoner in the orderly room (*Schreibstube),* who had been silent until now. "25 and SK. Out!" The latter was again aimed at me.

I clicked my heels.

"Prisoner 8214 is asking permission to leave,"

"Get out!"

Within the next moment, I was outside. Mechanically I registered at the gate and continued to walk towards the Block. I felt as if drunk. The unexpectedly harsh sentencing made me numb. I was so depressed that I could not think straight. Obtrusively, it was booming in my ears:

SK . . . SK . . . SK . . . (SK=Strafkompanie. Punishment Company, SK).

"You stupid dog!" I suddenly heard it yelled, and at the same moment, I felt a punch in my teeth. In a split second, I came to my senses . . .

In front of me stood the block leader (*Blockführer*), whom we called Tom Mix. When I passed by him, I had not taken off my cap, as was required by camp protocol.

"Prisoner 8214," I noisily introduced myself while I was clicking my wooden clogs.

"You surely are drunk, aren't you?" With a charming smile, he belted a second punch into my stomach, which threw me to the ground. However, I immediately forced myself to get up because I remembered that the SS men had the habit of kicking prisoners who were lying on the ground.

"I beg your pardon, but I didn't notice you because I have an important order from the reporting officer (*Rapportführer)* for the hospital barrack," I lied outrightly.

Tom Mix became more condescending.

"Well, that's certainly your luck, get lost!"

"I ask permission to leave!" I was already running away in a complete about-face.

At this point, I had really regained my senses and was coolheaded. When I had reached the Block, I crawled into the cellar and rolled myself a cigarette from the tobacco waste that I had found on the previous day. Now I could indeed deliberate more calmly and purposefully.

Well then, SK! . . .

What the entire camp considered more horrible than an execution: The Punishment Company! (SK) . . .

Instinctively, there arose before my mind's eyes the daily image of the people in the SK column as they were returning from work.

A long line of human shadows that came staggering on their legs and with their wooden clogs made the cobblestone pavement resound in marching step. At the end of the line, they always carried the victims of the day . . . corpses of those who had been shot to death, murdered, or beaten to death with clubs, or those who had, during work, died of "natural causes." And the marching step was drowned by the song of the Punishment Company (SK), "The blue dragons they are riding . . ." which they screamed out with their last strength.

As soon as this song started resounding, bit by bit the streets were deserted. For a too curious glance at the lines of the Punishment Company (SK), one could end up in there oneself . . .

During the following days, I ate. I ate in the camp as never before and as never afterwards. The block senior (*Blockältester*), actually a rather decent chap, relieved me from work for the rest of the days which still separated yet from the day on which I would be walking through the gate of the Punishment Company [SK]. The comrades slipped me some of their own meager portions. And in the evening, after the roll call, I was ordered to come to the block clerk, where a bucket of soup was awaiting me . . .

I ate. With cold calculation, I ate until I got stomach cramps. Whenever I became nauseated, I paused, lay down for one or two hours, and then continued to eat. Keep eating, eating as much as possible! . . .

About a week later, after the morning roll call, my number was called. A handshake from my comrades, a pat on the shoulder, an encouraging glance. "Hang in there!"

An hour later, accompanied by the camp senior (*Lagerältester*) and the *Blockführer*, I walked through the gate of Block Number 11.

In the square, which was enclosed by three high walls, there were three similarly convicted prisoners. Across from the stairs which led to the SK, there was a block which was used for beating. There was a wooden rack into which the feet would be placed; the upper part of the body would be placed on a special bench, whereby the buttocks were stretched outward.

The numbers were determined, and then we were lined up and we waited.

After a quarter of an hour, the command fell:

"Attention, eyes to the right!"

Fritzsch arrived in the square, accompanied by the camp physician, 1st Lieutenant, *SS-Obersturmführer* Entreß, and the *Rapportführer*.

There was a brief announcement: "Four prisoners have lined up for punishment."

Rapportführer Palitzsch opened the folder and called my number.

I jumped out of line as if pricked by a needle.

In a monotonous voice, *Rapportführer* Palitzsch read aloud to me the memorandum from which I learned that because of my acts of sabotage, which consisted of my stealing from the SS kitchen two mess tins filled with garbage, I was sentenced to twenty-five blows with a cane and to the Punishment Company (SK).

Immediately afterwards, *Blockführer* Gerlach ordered that I pull down my pants.

The camp physician cast an interested glance at my buttocks and noticed briefly,

"Healthy!"

Simultaneously, I tried to pull down my underwear together with my pants, but an energetic punch from Gerlach indicated that that was not allowed. One was permitted only to pull down the pants.

I placed my feet into the rack, lay down on the bench, and stretched my hands forward. These were seized by Bunker Foreman (*Bunkerkapo)* Kurt Pennewitz. He stretched me so tightly that it rattled in my bones.

I clenched my teeth and waited. In the meantime, *Blockführer* Gerlach tested the flexibility of the bullwhip.

"When he is beginning to whip you, then start to count out loudly!" Kurt suddenly whispered to me.

Only later did I realize how valuable this remark had been.

Indeed, the lashes were counted only from that moment when the one who was whipped himself began to count out loudly. Sometimes, he was given to understand only after the twentieth lash that he should begin the counting.

The few seconds that passed from the moment I was ready to receive the lashes until the moment I actually received the first whip, seemed longer to me than hours. It lasted incredibly long . . .

Finally.

Finally . . .

One . . . , a short, burning pain, as if scalded, as if stabbed. The pain is felt throughout my entire body. The fingertips, the skin on the shaven-bald head—everything is hellishly painful.

Two . . . Five . . .

The interval between one blow and the next seems like an eternity. As if they were lightning, my thoughts cross in my brain. Why doesn't he beat me? What is he waiting for? Does he indeed perhaps intend to finish me off with a shot to my neck???

Eight . . . Twelve . . .

Confused thoughts. Fear . . . Everything is already burning and pinching. Don't scream . . . And yet one would like to scream . . . Perhaps it would even be better to scream; then they might perhaps stop the beating?

Sixteen . . . Nineteen . . .

No! One may not scream. A few, who showed any weakness, were killed. One has to be stronger than one really is.

Twenty-two . . .

Still three . . . two . . . one blow!

"T w e n t y–f i v e!"

In this shout my entire pain discharged. But it sounded triumphantly!

I had not screamed, not even once.

Kurt Pennewitz let go of my hands.

"Now you'll have to report the reception of the punishment to the *Lagerführer*," he again whispered to me.

The feet which I pulled out of the rack were very heavy. It was difficult to place them together while standing to attention. But they closed nevertheless . . .

"Prisoner 8214 is reporting obediently to have received the punishment," I was able to say in one breath.

"Pull down your pants!"

The camp physician cast another glance at my behind.

"Okay. Bend your knees!"

After a quarter of an hour, I found myself in the cell of the Camp Bunker. It was the custom that the convicted prisoner was given three days of a more intensified arrest.

The stony floor cooled my burning buttocks wonderfully.

2

On the morning of the fourth day, the key rattled in the lock of the door. I got up and stood at attention.

When the door opened, a beam of light fell into the cell, which gave the broad-shouldered Private First Class (*SS-Rottenführer*), Gerlach, the appearance of a silhouette.

"Come!" . . .

On the stairs I was overcome by dizziness. Three days without any food or drink in a dark, moist cell which lacked any flow of air whatsoever had made me weaker than I thought. Only now, under the influence of the fullness of light and air, I felt how my muscles were shaking; with every step my knees gave in, it began to buzz in my ears, and a single cramp tightened my body.

I was unable to muster the strength to climb a few steps. Desperately I tried to hold on to the banister so that I would not fall down. Gerlach, who until now had been busy with the closing of the door, stood suddenly beside me . . .

"What is the matter?" His voice sounded terribly hostile. "Should someone perhaps help you?"

At that moment, when I saw his immense shoulders and his giant claws, I clearly remembered how I had witnessed some of the scenes in which he had badly mistreated the prisoners. I turned my eyes away from his unusually large, mirrorlike, polished, and studded boots, and I controlled myself. Fear proved to be stronger than weakness. With regained vitality, I climbed the rest of the stairs and walked through a door, into the corridor, and then I stopped.

"Into the *Schreibstube!*" he ordered.

The third door had a small sign marked *Schreibstube*.

Gerlach entered and, shortly thereafter, the clerk of the SK, prisoner Groell, came toward me.

With compassion, he looked at me . . .

"Are you a new arrival?"

"Yes."

"For what?"

I told him my story. Understandingly, he nodded his head.

"The most important thing is not to draw attention to yourself . . . You should always take care not to be the first or the last . . . And at work,"—he cast a significant glance at me— "you know how it is: Eyes and ears open! . . . "

He then took my personal data and assigned me to barrack-room number five.

"Report to the barrack-room senior!" (*Stubenälteste).*

Room number five was located on the first floor. I noticed that some prisoners were sitting in one corner. I approached them.

"Pardon me . . . I am a new arrival. To whom shall I report?"

"Reporting to Saint Peter would be best . . . ," responded one of those sitting there. He was a young, sturdy and strongly built lad with a beautiful but somehow strangely cheeky face . . . That was the *Stubenältester* in his very own person, the Ukraine, Bogdan Komaruicki. I learned later that he was the terror of the entire Company, a terrible sadist and degenerated human being.

"I will be going there, but in due time," I responded coldly. "But in the meantime, I am not in a hurry . . ."

"Shut up and don't talk so much . . . With us here such a kind doesn't live too long . . . How did you get caught?"

Once more I related my "offense."

"Phi . . . ," he waved his hand in refusal. "A weak organization. Do you have any cigarettes?"

"No, I have nothing. A while ago I was released from the Bunker . . ."

He reached into the cupboard.

"Here you have little wheels and thread . . . You should sow one little wheel into your blouse beneath the number, the other into the trouser . . . In a quarter of an hour you report to me."

"Yes, Sir!"

In the afternoon, I was already marching in some line of five toward the gravel pit where the SK was working. The column stopped on the spot. Foreman (*Kapo*) Johny yelled loudly:

"New arrivals, step out!"

Six of us stepped out. Two Germans, one Pole, one Czech, and two Jews.

We were scrutinized from top to toe.

Johny gave a brief "welcoming speech":

"You are in the Punishment Company (SK) . . . The good times are over. Here you will be sweating away your fat with which you have fattened yourself in the Camp . . . If you are obedient and diligent, then you might perhaps avoid the chimney. . . Reinhold!" he yelled at last.

A young chap with a green corner stepped out of the line.

"I am assigning to you these six men . . . retrain them accordingly . . . especially the Jews . . ."

"Yes, *Kapo*!"

He waved at us, and we marched towards a hut in front of which stood heavy iron carts which were lined up in a row.

"With me there is no walking," he announced even before we began to walk. "Back and forth in double trot. And if anyone should think that this might be too difficult, he can report to me . . ." All at once, he gave an unsuspecting Jew a blow with the handle of a shovel.

"Get on with it!"

We raced off like mad men. The path led through an open country which was extremely difficult to drive through. It was covered with grass and was very uneven. At the end of our column, Reinhold was running. Uninterruptedly, he was beating the last person in line with a club. I was exceptionally lucky because on the way there, I was not hit even once.

Finally we reached the pile of sand.

"Load up!" Reinhold's order rang out.

We seized the shovels. After a while, the carts were filled up; at least we thought so. Reinhold, however, was of a different opinion.

"You call that full?" The question was directed at a Jew and underlined with a blow of the club. An additional blow with the club made the Jew's bones crack. "Get down!"

The Jew did not understand what this was all about and let go of the cart. Once more there was a blow, this time to his head. There was a short shrill scream, and the beaten man fell down. Now Reinhold was seized by a real frenzy. He beat the man lying on the ground wherever he could hit him: on the head, in the stomach, on the chest, on the legs, on the fending-off hands; he beat him, as if he were out of his mind. With superhuman passion, he pounded upon him as forcefully as he could. Blood stained the yellow sand, and the body, which a minute ago still had had the form of a human being, resembled more, with every blow, a bleeding mass of flesh . . . The beaten man's resistance became weaker and weaker; his hands no longer protected his bleeding face; the screams gave way to a muffled moaning, but soon that too died away.

Not until now did Reinhold stop the beating. In the grass, he wiped off his club and took a deep sigh of relief. His face was red; his breathing was short. The wings of his nose quivered like the nostrils of a horse. Only then did he look at us.

"And you? . . . You are just standing there? . . . You lazy bunch!" He jumped at us like a rabid dog. The club, which was still warm, was dancing on our bones. This time I received two blows, but fortunately they were not very severe.

"Get on with it! . . . Two men carry this dog to the hut . . . The others follow me . . . But hurry . . ." He had not finished his sentence when we were already on our way.

Two of us who, were nearest to the murdered victim, carried the corpse in front of the hut. There was a provisional cemetery. There were days when after the whistle blow which announced the end of the work day, thirty, at times forty, victims of the day were at this cemetery.

In the meantime, the three of us pushed forward the carts with an immense effort; they were filled half a meter higher than was usually the case. I felt a severe pain in my feet and it was as if my hands were ripped off my arms. But just keep going, still faster! . . .

The area of the countryside seemed to have conspired against us. Ditches, small hills, grass . . . everything stood in the way of the iron cart wheels which bored deeper and deeper into the ground.

Every stop meant new blows. Ali Kwasigroch from Danzig had just received ten penalizing strokes with the cane, when the wheel of my cart bored so deeply into the clay soil that I had to stop. Immediately Reinhold was at my side . . .

"You are surely taking a break, are you not?"

I clenched my teeth and pushed the cart forward with all my strength. The cart, however, began to sway, and before I could prevent it, it was lying on the heap of the sand which had already been tipped out. Reinhold whistled with sheer satisfaction,

"You stupid dog . . ." and he belted a blow to my back with a cane. "You are sabotaging the work . . . You spilled the sand so that you could take a rest . . . A second blow hit my arm, which fell down, as if lame.

"Bend down!"

Immediately, I bent down and stretched out my buttocks. From my experience in the camp, I knew that the rear end was the most resistant part of the body.

The pain which I felt from the first blow was incredible. My muscles were still swollen from the first twenty-five blows; they were extremely hard and sensitive. The blows which were now hitting me resulted in pain beyond all description. It was as if a scalding, a burning stabbing, ran through my entire body, and that caused me to be so hot that it could not be held back. Immediately, I was steaming with sweat.

"Get up!" I heard it ordered. I had "only" received fifteen strokes. From the back it ran down my legs.

"You smell, you stupid pig," Reinhold remarked. He added, "I give you ten minutes so that you can clean up."

I clicked my heels, and in the next moment I was already in the latrine. The cleaning up took only five minutes. The other five minutes I sat in the grass and massaged my overexerted behind.

Before lunch break, Reinhold had "finished off" yet a second Jew. In our group there were now only four left.

The work tempo, however, was now obviously slowing down. We now drove by ourselves because our work foreman (*Vorarbeiter*) participated in the hunt for Jews which was organized at the chain of guards. This was a popular pastime of Edelhardt, the commando leader (*Kommandoführer)* of the SK.

This game was as follows: The working area was surrounded by a chain of guards which consisted of SS men. The guards were instructed to shoot any prisoner who attempted to trespass the chain of guards. *Kommandoführer* Edelhardt chose daily several prisoners, especially Jews, whom he entrusted to the special care of the *Vorarbeiter,* who were of Reinhold's kind. They beat up the "chosen" ones with canes until they ran in despair into the chain of guards. The guards were, of course, initiated into the "program of the game." They waited until the runners were a few meters away from them, and then they shot down the "fugitives" like rabbits. After that, the guard was given three days of special leave because he had prevented the "escape" of a prisoner. And the family of the prisoner received the news that their loved one had been killed while trying to escape. On days when new transports of Jews arrived, the number of those "killed while escaping" increased to fifty.

Thus, the first day in the Punishment Company (SK) passed. After a blow of the whistle, all groups formed a column. The survivors and the dead were counted. The prisoners of the last row took the corpses on their shoulders, and *Kapo* Johny, who placed himself at the head of the line, gave the order:

"March in step! . . . Sing!"

The wooden clogs crashed on the bricks and the song, "The blue dragons they are riding . . ." penetrated into heaven.

The evening roll call was exceptionally brief; it lasted only an hour; thereafter we went into our barrack-rooms. Our daily rations consisted of hot, brown-colored water, a portion of bread which had been significantly shortened to the advantage of the *Kapos* and *Vorarbeiter* and did not exceed the weight of 200 grams, a microscopic portion of margarine with which one could, with some skill, smear a half slice of bread. At lunchtime, we received about three quarters of a liter soup; that is, water in which some beats or slices of stems and leaves were swimming; only the lucky ones also found a potato in it once in a while.

Since the beginning of my camp existence, I was used to rationing the bread for the morning and evening. But on this day, I devoured everything all at once. Then I reclined carefully into my bed. My neighbor was Ali Kwasigroch from Danzig. During work, Reinhold had turned a head even more on him than on me.

It was not until now that I became fully aware of the experiences of the day. The hard bed, which I was used to, now seemed to be laid out with bricks. My body hurt with the slightest movement; my heart pounded fast; the fever began to rise . . . I fully realized that I could survive the next day if I were able to rise early and, furthermore, that I would be able to work the entire day.

I realized that my muscles, which had been smashed to beefsteak with Reinhold's club, were as hard as stone. Therefore, it would be out of the question that I would be able to work . . .

Carefully, I began to massage. Ali did the same.

In the silence of the night, while it was entirely dark in the hall, we kneaded our smashed bodies meticulously for a long time.

Suddenly, I heard the one from Danzig whisper:

"Listen . . ."

"Yes. What?"

"It would be good if at the end, we were to apply compresses . . ."

"The room is locked. We can't get into the washroom . . ."

"Hm . . ."

There was silence again. After a while, I heard steps and soon thereafter a typical noise near the bucket.

"Ali!"

"Yes, what?"

"Do you hear it?"

"What?"

"Someone is pouring into the bucket. We have water . . ."

"Are you crazy?" . . . However, he seemed to think it over, and after a while he added, "Perhaps you are right, after all!"

I waited a few minutes until the prisoner in question had finished his business. Then I glided carefully down from the bed, with a towel in hand.

I was extraordinarily lucky because until now only those who were concerned with "small matters" had gone to the bucket.

I soaked Ali's and my towels, wrung them out, and returned to my bed,

The cool, acidic compress had a wonderful effect on the inflamed muscles. It smelled a bit, but it helped marvelously. . .

During the night I changed the compresses several times.

3

THE COMMAND OF THE *Stubendienst* woke me up.

"Get up!"

As fast as I could, I slipped out of bed and went into the overcrowded washroom. It was a small room with twelve faucets. Over one hundred prisoners pushed around them and waited while the "VIPs"—*Kapos* and *Vorarbeiter*—took their time finishing their morning toilet. They were, however, not in a hurry. Slowly and carefully, they lathered themselves with good toilet soap, savored the pleasure of the lathering for a long time, soaped once more and again rinsed it off. A "Pipel"—a young male servant and prostitute for the *Kapos*—who was already waiting nearby with a terry towel, rubbed the refreshed dignitary dry. Only after that was the faucet turned over to the "rabble." Then the fight for the water faucet began. Every prisoner tried hard to at least give the impression that he had ducked his trunk into the water because the *Stubendienst* stood at the doors of the barrack rooms and checked those who entered. Anyone who was not wet enough was zapped on the spot twenty-five times . . .

Miraculously, I succeeded in getting to the faucet and was able to hold my neck and chest under the refreshing jets of water. Happy and wet, I paraded in front of Komarnicki, who did not even notice me. I received my coffee and was about to drink it when the gong which signaled the lineup for the work detachment (*Arbeitskommando*) resounded. Our *Stubendienst* seemed as if struck by lightning.

"Move, everybody out!"

With one jump, he reached the nearest prisoners. The screams of those he maltreated mixed with the muffled blows of the club. Everyone rushed to the door in order to reach the corridor.

There stood the *Kapos* and *Vorarbeiter,* of course, with heavy clubs and their fists.

"Faster! Tempo! . . . Move on! . . . Get going!" sounded from all sides. The mass of the prisoners reached the stairs. Somebody fell. Over him another, over this one again others. The revolving living ball rolled down the stairs—cursing, moaning, pleading, screaming, rumbling, banging.

"Move on! . . . Move on! . . . Faster!!!"

Finally we are in the square. Three or four of those who were crushed were carried to the washroom located on the ground floor.

"Man in front! . . . Line up!" Again there were screams. This time they came from the *Blockältesten,* and their helpers. The *Stubendienste* are running through the rooms as if possessed. Someone did not quite correctly line up. Bum! The clubs worked over all of his body parts which were extending over the line. Feet, hands, head; it does not matter where he hits. Everything is so fast, like streaks of lightning, as if in a mania.

"Counting!" the command of the *Blockältesten* is ringing out. At number nineteen, someone has counted incorrectly. It is a foreigner, who is not familiar with the counting in German. The *Stubendienste* rush to him like hyenas, and already they had dragged him out of the line. One kicked him; the other hit him with the club. "Into the washroom with him!"

"Counting!"

This time it works out; but the position is not correct. For a change, there is one too many. Again a running around; again the clubs are in motion. It turned out that the congruence was very poor. Everything is repeated . . . Finally . . .

"Block 11 . . . Stand to Attention! . . . Caps Off! . . . Eyes to the right!"

The *Blockälteste*, holding the *Rapportbuch* in his right hand, his cap in his left hand, is coming from the front of the Company to the gate where *Blockführer* Gerlach has just appeared . . . A short report. Gerlach is scrutinizing everything. Slowly, he is inspecting the lines and is counting very accurately. He is looking into everyone's face; this one he is hacking, another one he is hitting, and then he is moving on, dignified and full of himself. He has completed the checking of the count. Indifferently, he is looking into the book, comparing it. It is correct. Slowly, he is moving to the gate; he is walking through it to the appeal center of the camp in order to give a report to the *Rapportführer*, who is officiating at the desk.

And in the meantime, we are standing. Straight. To attention, our heads turned to the right, motionlessly, almost not breathing. The *Blockälteste*, the

Stubendienste, and the *Kapos* circle between the rows, observing the slightest motion. One is not allowed to move a limb; one may not rest; not even coughing is allowed.

Someone is coughing just now. A short while later, he is already screaming . . . And again he is silent . . . This is lasting for about a quarter of an hour. Finally Gerlach is returning. He turned the Rapportbuch over to the *Blockältesten* . . . Finished . . .

"Eyes straight forward! . . . Move! . . ."

Pfum . . . It all passed luckily . . .

"Work detail (*Arbeitskommando*), stand to attention! . . . "

Again movement. We fall into line for the march, rows of five. Three hundred human beings, all are running over the place in the small square. Everyone is looking for his row of five . . .

And again clubs . . . Finally, we are standing. We are standing like this for a good half hour, ready to march out.

Finally it is said:

"In step! . . . Forward march! . . . Sing! . . ."

"The blue dragoons, they are riding! . . ."

I am marching in a row of five together with Ali. During the night, we had become somewhat stronger. I feel strong enough, but my behind is hurting; it is unbearable. From time to time, I palpate my body. Everything is swollen, hard, but the fever has subsided. Maybe phlegm will now not develop even though it is almost always a consequence of heavy blows . . . On the way, we pass by the Commandos of the Camp (work detachments), who are ready to march. I notice that some comrades are carefully searching for me in the rows . . . Someone is unnoticeably waving at me.

"Hang in there!"

I do what I can . . . We walk through the gate, and after a quarter of an hour, we have reached the gravel pit. On command, we run in all directions, each one to his group. I belong to Reinhold . . . The process by which one is added to the "new arrivals" is lasting for a week . . . Maybe I'll make it through the day . . . I am very hopeful . . . We seize the carts. The number of "new arrivals" has increased. Some of the older ones had been transferred to us for disciplinary reasons. Reinhold is obviously in a bad mood. He is cursing more often than yesterday . . . That is a bad sign!

I was the first one to push the cart, cautiously and carefully. Don't push too fast because this will exhaust too much energy, and don't go too slowly because Reinhold . . . He is already beating up someone . . . This time it is a Czech. We are just pushing along the edge of the gravel pit. A meter to the right—there is a slope. And there is a hole about fifteen meters deep . . . That gives Reinhold a new idea . . .

"You pig!" he screams. "I shall show you how to push . . .!" He seized the cart out of the startled Czech's hands and topped out the sand. "Get into the cart! . . ."

The Czech stands there undecidedly. However, the club of the *Vorarbeiter* is helping him to make a decision. Cautiously he steps into the cart. With ease Reinhold is lifting the load. He takes a run-up into the direction of the hole, and he is letting the cart with its contents plunge into the hole . . . We hear a terrible scream, a rumbling . . . and . . .

"Well done, Reinhold! . . ." The *Kommandoführer* is patting him on the shoulders with satisfaction . . . "Here, you have some cigarettes . . ."

The face of the young henchman is beaming. The cigarettes disappear quickly into his pockets.

"Yes, *Kommandoführer!*" fell his short answer. It sounded like the barking of a dog.

"Get on with it!"

We continued to push. Near a certain pile of sand, the car of the camp is parking. *Vorarbeiter* Gerhard stands near it. During better times, I had given him some soup once in a while. Surprised, he looked at me.

"Man, how do you look?"

I point towards Reinhold.

"Pst . . ."

He waved his hand aside.

"He can do to me somewhere . . ." followed by an indicative motion of his hand.

"Who has beaten you up like that?"

"He over there!"

"Wait . . . Listen . . ."

Gerhard takes Reinhold aside. They talk about something, and, after a while, I hear my number.

"Prisoner 8214," I reported.

"Shut up!" Reinhold looked inquisitively at Gerhard. "That one?"

"Yes!"

"You come to me during the lunch hour every day." He turned to me. "And now leave the cart and come with me . . ." Without looking at me further, he goes forward. Gerhard squeezes about ten cigarettes and a piece of bread into my hand.

Until lunchtime, I work at the sieve. I throw the loosely hacked gravel on it with a shovel. The finer gravel falls to one side, along with the sand; the coarser gravel falls to the other side.

What a royal job!!!

I am happy; I see the sun and hardly feel any pain. I shovel mechanically and let my thoughts wander.

The noon gong.

After I had gulped down my miserable soup, I run immediately to the hut. Reinhold is noticing me. He is bringing me a full bowl of soup.

"Here is your grub . . . , and if Gerhard has deceived me, then you better watch out . . ." After saying this, he nodded his head significantly.

"What do you mean by deceiving?"

"He has promised me twenty cigarettes weekly for you."

I was frightened. Twenty cigarettes, that was an enormous capital in the camp. I reached into my pocket . . .

"I have just a few for you here," I said, and I gave him the gift which I had just received a short while ago.

Without a word, he put them into his pocket. But when he walked away, he muttered briefly,

"Okay!"

I still retained him.

"However, I have still another favor to ask you."

"What's that?"

"My friend Ali is working with you. Perhaps you could let him work at my sieve . . ."

"Who is he?"

"The tall one from Danzig."

"Good."

After lunch I worked with Ali. Toward evening, the news spread among us that during the course of the day, a transport of Jews had arrived in the Punishment Company (SK) from the recently conquered city of Lemberg. Therefore, the work ended half an hour earlier. After that the *Kommandoführer* ordered a lineup of the *Kapos*, the *Vorarbeiter* and all prisoners who had a green corner on their outfit, which means the professional criminals. At the end he gave a brief speech:

"Because of good behavior you have been appointed *Vorarbeiter*. I do not have to explain to you what your duty is. You had time and opportunity enough to acquaint yourselves with it during your stay in the camp. The Jews are the ones whose supervisors you will be. In my commando, I only want to have Aryans . . . Understood?"

"Yes! Certainly!" It resounded in one voice.

After that we went into the camp. The new VIPs were already carrying the badges of their power: Clubs . . . After we arrived in the square of the SK, we were lined up separately near the gate while Gerlach called the *Blockältesten*. Immediately following came the order:

"New arrivals to line up for roll call."

No one knew what that meant. This was, after all, the first roll call in these people's lives. Confused, they circled around in the square and did not know where and how they should line up.

Gerlach smiled with satisfaction and gave a signal to the *Blockältesten*. He in turn signaled to the *Stubendienst* and to the *Vorarbeiter*.

Like a pack of hounds, they rushed towards the unsuspecting newcomers. The clubs circled through the air and bounced off their heads. An indescribable shrieking and confusion began. Five hundred people began running around in the square, as if mad. They began to bounce into each other; they began to trample on those who had fallen to the ground, only trying to escape from the enraged VIPs. This worked according to the instructions of the "strategist" Gerlach. Within a space of a few meters, they drove everything forward, dealing blows right and left.

The Jews, who were separated from those at the other part of the square by the chain of those who did the beating, began to back up against the wall. They were finally so crowded together that even those who had been beaten were unable to get out of the way. And now something sinister took place. . . .

Those who had been beaten and who were nearest to the *Vorarbeiter* began, in a dreadful fright, to climb upon the shoulders of those standing in front of them. Those in turn reached for the next, knocked them down, and climbed over their bodies, higher and higher. What emerged here was something like an eerie, swaying, living wall of bodies that screamed to heaven and was groaning terribly, and on top, it was moving unsteadily . . . That lasted for about a quarter of an hour. Finally, *Rottenführer* Gerlach began to whistle, still sneering, an image of sheer satisfaction.

The group who had done the beating retreated, puffing and panting, soiled with blood.

"Enough for today . . . *Blockältester*!" Gerlach turned to Hans. "The *Vorarbeiter* receive a triple ration of bread today as a bonus for their heavy labor." He laughed at his own joke. "And now get ready for the roll call!"

On this evening, thirty-seven dead people were carried into the washroom. They had been inhumanly massacred. Those who were still alive despite their condition were declared unfit for work and were butchered by the *Stubendienst* and the *Vorarbeiter*. . .

4

One day they retained us longer than usual. The *Blockälteste* Hans told us that today an order from the *Lagerführer* would be read to us. However, no one knew what he meant by that.

After we had waited for half an hour, *Blockführer* Gerlach appeared in the square. He accepted the report and moved to the center in front of the housing block.

"Everyone listen! . . . As of today, for every escaped prisoner ten other prisoners will be executed. If the escape occurs in camp, ten of those prisoners who live in the same block as the escapee will be held responsible. If the escape should occur at the work place, then that number among the group in which the escapee had worked will be executed. The selection will be carried out in person by the *Lagerführer* . . ." At this point, Gerlach paused briefly and let his gaze roam around us, whereupon he continued, "This ordinance applies to the general camp. . . . Concerning the Punishment Company (SK), the *Lagerführer* has increased the number so that not ten, but rather twenty, prisoners will receive the death penalty!" These last words were spoken with obvious satisfaction. "And now the second part: It has been announced that an entire family of an escaped prisoner has been arrested and will be brought into the local camp and will be executed. Any property will be confiscated for the benefit of the German Reich!"— again a short pause. This time, however, Gerlach paused somewhat longer. He lit a cigarette, drew a few puffs and added of his own accord, "You are informed now, are you not? For every single one, twenty men. . . . And the *Lagerführer* is of the opinion that the bullets are more important for the war on the front, and the gallows are too expensive. Therefore, he has decided that those who are selected for the execution will be locked up in the Hunger

Bunker. They will get nothing to eat and to drink until they die a wretched death. Has everyone understood?"

"Yes, Sir!" It resounded in unison from about five hundred throats.

"Dismissed!"

We went into the Block and discussed this ordinance. We did not worry about it because the SK was so heavily guarded that an escape was almost impossible. Since the camp existed, no prisoner had fled the Punishment Company (SK). . . . In the camp, however, it happened recently quite often.

The following days passed quickly. They resembled each other in their terrible uniformity. Early wake-up, washing, coffee reception; then roll call, departure and work—a number of unlucky ones who were beaten up and a few deaths—then lunch. After lunch again work until the gong, and in the meantime a "variety of changes" as part of the routine: marching back to the camp, a longer or shorter roll call, coffee reception, and sleeping. And every day, all that started anew without any particular changes.

One day our column was regrouped. That happened to my disadvantage. Instead of working at the sieve, which I had done until now, I was assigned to the group which carried brushwood. Our *Vorarbeiter*, Willi Mengler from Saxony, behaved decently although he carried a club, according to orders, as did all the others; he very rarely used it, however. Counting the *Vorarbeiter*, there were twenty men in our group. Until noon, work proceeded smoothly. I was even content because with this work time passed much faster than before. We ate our food, and during our spare time, we talked as usual about our food. Everyone related what he really would like to eat now and cited his favorite dish from his time of freedom. Thus, the lunch break passed.

After lunch, we continued with the same work. From time to time, Willi permitted someone to go to the latrine. . . . And because Stanislaw Nowaczyk, prisoner no. 8505, suffered from diarrhea, which was quite common in the camp, no one was surprised when he remained for three quarters of a day in the lavatory. Immediately after lunch, he asked Willi for permission to leave, and then he ran quickly in the direction of the latrine. A quarter of an hour, a half hour, three quarters of an hour passed—Nowaczyk did not return. . . . The concerned *Vorarbeiter* sent one of the prisoners to check it out. . . . We were all convinced that our sick one had become so weak that he simply did not have the strength to return. After a while, the messenger returned. Nowaczyk was not in the lavatory.

Willi ran immediately to *Kapo* Johny; he was as pale as all of us were. Shortly after that, we heard a whistle, which was immediately followed by the orders . . .

"Company, line up!"

Upon such a command, every prisoner threw his tools to the ground and ran as fast as he could to the square for the roll call. We lined up in groups.

The *Kapos* and the *Kommandoführer* began the counting. Nineteen of us men were immediately separated from the rest and entrusted to the care of three strange *Vorarbeiter*. In the meantime, the working area of the SK was immediately searched. After half an hour, every corner and every bush had been probed. Nowaczyk was nowhere to be found. There was not the slightest doubt that he had escaped.

Now the entire madness of the *Kapo* and the *Kommandoführer* vented upon us. First, everyone received twenty-five strokes with a cane, and everything else had to be left to pure chance. I was obviously lucky because no one had to help me when returning to the camp. The others had to be carried. . . . During the roll call our group was positioned in a special lineup. After approximately half an hour, the shrill shout of the *Blockältesten* rang out: "Attention!" and Fritzsch, accompanied by several noncommissioned officers (*SS Unteroffiziere)*, came into the square. For a while, he was talking with *Blockführer* Gerlach, and then he approached us.

Willi reported the fact of the escape. Immediately, he was punched in the teeth, whereupon Fritzsch gave a short speech:

"According to the order of the High Command of the SS (SS *Reichsführer)*, Himmler, you are all sentenced to death . . . understood?"

"Yes, Sir!"

He nodded briefly towards Gerlach and went away. We, however, were given the command: "To the right! . . . In double line, forward march!"

Everything went so fast that we did not even have the time to reflect on the matter. Three minutes later, we were already in the Bunker. There were ten men in one cell and nine in the other. I belonged to the nine men cell.

The cell was dark, without windows. On the ceiling there was a small opening through which air could come in. Inside there was twilight. After a few minutes, however, the eyes adjusted to it. We sat down on the concrete floor.

My fellow sufferers were the Pole Brodacki from Neu-Sandez, the German Konrad Merschel from East Prussia, the German Willi Mengler from Saxony, the Czech Dr. Sinkowicz from Prague, and the Poles Josef Kowalczyk and Heinrich Stanko from Warsaw. I did not know the names of the other two.

During the first hour, we all spoke about our fate. Now what?

Would this indeed be the end? Perhaps something might change yet. These and other questions swirled in confusion through the air, but no one had an answer. Finally, it became silent. Every one of us was absorbed in his own thoughts.

I was the first one, and therefore, I was lying close to the door. For a long time, I was unable to think. A host of ideas seized me. All culminated in one thought: Is there still any hope?

Logically considered, there was none. I had been in the camp for too long to believe in a sudden miracle. There were no miracles here. . . . We were sentenced to death, and there was no power in the whole world that could have rescued us. There were only a few days left, the number of which depended on the strength of the organism, and then the end would follow. . . .

I changed my position and lay on my back. It was already completely dark in the cell. The silence which ruled here was unbearable.

If they would only execute us! This hopeless waiting was indeed the worst thing. The stomach, which was used to taking in food around this time, began to make itself felt. It was pulling together and began to grumble. . . . Just then, it became frightfully clear to me: I shall never eat again. This realization tormented me like an annoying bluebottle and took root in my consciousness. Never again . . . Neither a piece of bread nor a drop of water . . . Nothing!

And right now, upstairs around this time, five hundred people are eating. Thousands of my own kind in the camp are leaning over their mess tins with coffee and bite into aromatic bread . . .

What might they serve with the bread today? Thursday . . . On this day they really get margarine and jam . . . as sweet as sugar. They spread it on the bread and bite into it. . . . Damn it!

And outside the camp at the same time, millions of people are eating. In elegant restaurants, polite waiters dressed in frocks move between the tables. How may I help you? Perhaps you would like a cold plate? Perhaps fish? Roast meat? We have an excellent partridge in cream? . . . or perhaps a raw beefsteak with onions and French fries, dripping with fat?

I feel how dry my throat is, how hot my lips are, and how my saliva is steadily thickening. From time to time I swallow it. I have to use the saliva carefully. If I swallow everything, well, that's all nonsense!

But starving to death and dying of thirst; that must be horrible. . . . Somewhere in a sensational novel, I read a description of it. The hero of the novel had been locked up in a cellar where he remained for several days without any food and drink. Luckily, at the last minute, an ingenious detective found him. . . .

That was possible in a novel. But neither a detective nor anything else will help me. How was the description again? First comes the pain—instinctively I touch my stomach with my hand. Nothing can be felt there yet. Nothing is hurting yet. . . .

Then comes the fever . . . buzzing in the ears . . . light sleep . . .

And later—death!

That would not be too bad. In reality it must be much worse! The author of the novel had no imagination, or he had never been hungry. . . .

"Colleague!" I suddenly hear my neighbor whisper.

"What is the matter?"

"Do you think there are still any chances?" I realize how the voice of the questioner is reaching for an affirmative answer. I am seized by anger. . . . A woman, damn it. He is whimpering already after the first hour. I've got to bring him to reason.

"Chances? For what?" I asked stupidly.

"Yes, you know! Will we ever get out of here?"

I laughed out loud.

"We will leave this cell, in any case. They will carry us out, colleague!" I answered with complete satisfaction. He sighed loudly.

"That is simply horrible! You know, my wife wrote in her last letter that she had borne me a son. I have never seen him." His voice seemed to give in; it was trembling that badly. "I counted on it that I would somehow persevere . . . and . . . then I would see . . . the boy . . ."

I am getting nauseated. . . . I feel a strange cramp in my throat, a warm moisture under my eyelids . . . Because I too . . . In the darkness, I am tapping my neighbor on the shoulder.

"Perhaps they will let us out yet," I said spontaneously, and at the same time, I realize that this sudden change of mind must sound incredibly stupid.

As an answer, I heard a soft sobbing. I turned my back toward him and tried to fall asleep.

Then someone in the back is beginning to pray loudly. The soft voice is vibrating strangely through the acoustic cell. There is a supernatural sound to it. The words of the prayers which we know so well from our childhood acquire another meaning. . . .

"And forgive us our debt as we forgive our debtors . . ."

Perhaps for the first time in my life, I reflected on the meaning of these words. . . . Should we forgive? . . .

I revolt against it . . . I shall not forgive . . . At the same time, I had to think about the fact that it will still take a very long time until my debtors will be judged. For the time being, they go about freely, they eat, drink, smoke and are certainly far from asking for the forgiveness of their debt. . . . But I am very much inclined to do it.

When I ask for forgiveness of my debt, then I myself must forgive . . . Eye for an eye . . . that is really very logical. . . . Someone begins to sing. After a while, the second, third, fifth join him . . . The entire cell roars with the song "I was to wit in the Camp of Auschwitz . . . "

Was I? Was I? I still am. Several days, I still am . . . They change the melody: "With me you are beautiful. . . ." Total madness!

I close my ears. The leaping rhythm of the fox-trot drives me crazy. But I control myself. Perhaps others are in need of something like this just now. . . .

The song is over; new silence. It is even more oppressive than before.

I get up and start walking up and down the cell. In the darkness, I step on someone's foot.

"Could you be more careful?" I heard an irritated voice say. "He has picked the right place and time to take a walk. . . . "

The man was right. I lay down again.

Long after midnight, I fall asleep.

The next day passes without any special incidents. Without interruption, we tell each other very different stories simply to not have to think about reality. Dr. Sinkowicz does not speak a word the entire day. He does not participate in our conversations and is lying continually on his back with his eyes closed. . . . The most cheerful of all is Stanko, a young chap about twenty years of age with beautiful blue eyes and blond hair. He tells jokes off the cuff, he sings for us, and he re-enacts how different dances are danced in the suburbs of Warsaw. That is really funny. Finally he too is tired; he is lying down on the ground and closes his eyes.

And again it is silent. The first twenty-four hours have passed. I am really anxious to see how long one can endure this. For the time being, it was not too bad yet.

During the night, however, my condition turns serious. From time to time I moisten my lips. In a flash they are dry again. I begin to have a fever. That is bad.

I pass the night without any sleep. In the morning it was even worse. Indeed, I felt a strong buzzing in my ears. The author of the book was right after all. . . .

Again we are all silent. About midday, the German, Konrad Merschel, is getting up and is beginning to bang at the door. Nobody is trying to stop him. Perhaps they might indeed open the door?

After a few minutes, he stops. Resigned, he reclined next to the door and curses loudly.

"What do you want?" Willi asks him.

"To the *Lagerführer* . . . I am going to enlist as a volunteer in the SS. It is crazy to lose one's life because of such a dumb matter. I am twenty-three years old."

"Pig!" Willi assesses briefly and cuts the conversation. Willi has a red corner on his outfit. He was once upon a time a functionary of the SPD (Social Democratic Party) in Saxony.

"It is easy for you to say, 'Pig'! You are over forty years old, but I have had nothing from life yet."

"Why are you incarcerated?" Willi asked after a while.

"Thefts . . . and a robbery."

Willi is laughing.

"Why did you unofficially rob? You should have entered the SS straightaway. By now, you could have already been commandant of Auschwitz and would be able to kill officially. . . ." He is still looking at him for a while. Then he turns to us. "Those are the worst kind. In order to live they sell their own child. Yuck!" He spits contemptuously and finally turns his back to Merschel.

Toward the evening of the third day, Dr. Sinkowicz is beginning to vomit. Tears pour out of his eyes; convulsions are shaking his entire body.

We are trying to help him, but he pushes us away with both hands. We later learned that during the previous night, while all of us were asleep, Dr. Sinkowicz had been breaking a metal spoon into small pieces and then swallowed all of them in the hope that with such help, he might be able to accelerate his death. He had been able to smuggle the metal spoon into the cell.

I could not sleep until the early morning. The condition of the Czech worsens continually. He now has a high fever and is vomiting blood at regular intervals.

The two men from Warsaw are now occupied with something very odd. They tear their leather boots into small pieces. They carefully separate the leather from the cloth and divide it into new little piles.

As it later turned out, Stanko too had recalled a novel whose hero had extended his life by chewing leather.

Toward noon, the small pieces of leather, which had been soaked in shoe polish and sweat, were solemnly divided among us.

I have no courage to eat this stuff and I am waiting for the others. Those who had suggested this began.

Not even a quarter of an hour had passed when there were already signs of the consequences. Both started to have terrible pain. They yelled and screamed and doubled over in anguish. Then the vomiting followed.

Around midnight the Czech met his end. . . . We carried him to the other side of the cell. Over his pale face, soiled with blood, spread a wonderful peace. . . .

This was the first one!

In the evening, Merschel had a nervous breakdown. He jumped to the door and worked it over with his hands while he was screaming incomprehensibly. After a few minutes, foam appeared on his lips and he lost consciousness. Something similar happened to Stanko. He walked about in the cell until he was seized by a cramp and fell head-on onto the stony floor so that the cell resounded.

The fifth day . . . I am incredibly weak. The pain subsided somewhat but I am terribly thirsty. It is buzzing in my ears. I cannot stand it. Every noise in the cell causes a physical pain in my head, as if caused by a blow.

I am indifferent to all that is happening around me. For a few hours now I have my eyes closed and do not have the strength to open them. And for what? I am still thinking very clearly but very slowly. Now I am even having difficulties recognizing my surroundings. The buzzing develops into a dominant sensation. I do not feel anything else. A strange paralysis seizes me. I am breathing rapidly.

For a long time, I am lying like this. I don't know for how long. The thoughts are hardly reaching my consciousness. I do not know anything any longer, and I do not understand anything anymore.

Suddenly, I am getting very hot. I am falling somewhere into the depths. For a short moment, I am regaining my consciousness. That seems already the end. I am dying. It is really not so terrible. . . . That was my last thought. A terrible cold awakened me. I opened my eyes and closed them immediately. At first I did not see anything except for a stream of light which hurt my eyes. . . .

"Come on! Get up!"

I understood that, but I did not move in order to get up. It simply did not want to enter my head. . . .

I felt how someone lifted me up and how I was suddenly immersed in a flood of light and air.

Again I opened my eyes. I was lying in the square of the SK, and Kurt Pennewitz, the *Stubendienst* Wacek, and someone else were bending over me. My fellow sufferers from the cell were lying next to me. Of course, only those who were still alive. . . .

Something was poured into my mouth, something divinely wet and warm. I drank as if mad, and as I swallowed, I began to feel better.

"That's enough for now," I heard Wacek's voice saying.

"The next."

After about an hour, I had regained consciousness inasmuch as I could already hear and understand everything.

I looked at my neighbors. There were fourteen of us in the square.

"We have to lay them down in two rows. I see no other alternatives." I suddenly heard the voice of the *Blockältesten*, and I felt that they were carrying me to the other side. Thus, we were now lying in two rows, each consisting of seven men.

The sun was shining directly into my eyes. Despite this, my teeth were chattering with cold. After a while, I heard someone yell "Attention! "and I saw Fritzsch entering the square, accompanied by the *Rapportführer.*

For a while, he stopped at the *Blockältesten*, and then he came toward us. He scrutinized all of us critically and decided, "The first row to the Block, the second back to the Bunker."

"There are already seven corpses in there," Kurt Pennewitz remarked, "and five dead ones are already lying below there."

"Ah. But it does not matter. The last two men of the first row to follow." He nodded and departed in the direction of the gate.

Later, when I was in the barrack room, the *Stubendienst* told me that a letter had arrived from Berlin with the order that ten men were to be released from the Bunker. Indeed, Himmler's order had mentioned that only ten were to be included in the retaliatory criminal proceedings. Fritzsch, however, on his own authority, had this order increased for the SK.

The next days passed like a fairy tale. The ten of us were the darlings of everybody from the *Blockführer* Gerlach down to the most vicious *Vorarbeiter.* We received from the *Blockältesten*—I do not know whence it came—organized milk, and on Saturday Gerlach presented us with a bottle of rum, and in addition each one of us received a pack of cigarettes. . .

"Such luck as you had, I myself would like to have," he said while he presented us with the gifts. He also relieved us from work for two weeks.

The five fellow prisoners who had the bad luck to have been at the head of the second row were carried from the Bunker to the mortuary two days later.

5

Eight days later, the *Blockälteste* Hans ordered a lineup of all prisoners who were present in the Block. Counting the *Stubenältesten* about twenty persons gathered together. Hans scrutinized our emaciated figures critically, nodding, and said:

"I need a few strong people for work, but nothing can be done with you. Which of you wants to earn 'extra soup'?"

Since I felt somewhat better, I stepped forward as the first out of line. Then four additional men volunteered. We were added to the group of the *Stubenältesten*.

"Wait in the washroom for further directions," *Blockältester* Hans said abruptly.

The washroom, which was located on the ground floor, was a small room with a window which led into the square.

"Today 'Wilhelm Tell' will appear again," *Stubenältester* Wacek remarked. We listened attentively with interest. The executioner of the death sentences, *SS-Hauptscharführer* Palitsch, was known in the camp as "Wilhelm Tell."

"Is something due again?"

Wacek nodded.

"Yesterday the family of the prisoner who had escaped from the construction area was brought in. There are five people altogether."

There was silence.

"Well, the guests are gathering," the boilerman Bronek, who stood near the window, said suddenly.

We moved closer.

Several men in uniform appeared in the square: *Lagerführer* Fritzsch, SS physician Entreß, Corporal (*SS-Unterscharführer*) Stark, work detail leader (*Arbeitsdienstführer*) Heßler, and *Rapportführer* Palitzsch. The last one carried a sport gun in his right hand.

"Move away from the window!" Wacek ordered. "These gentlemen don't like to be watched."

At that moment, the door opened and we heard Hans calling out:

"Four men and the boilerman. But hurry!"

The four men who were standing nearest and Bronek disappeared behind the door. Three men still remained. We moved away from the window a bit but only far enough so that we could clearly see everything that was happening outside.

The men in uniform talked with each other. They were smoking and listening to Fritzsch. From time to time, they were roaring with laughter. Palitzsch leaned on his gun and drew circles into the soft soil. Then Gerlach approached the group and reported something. Fritzsch nodded affirmatively. The conversation broke off. Palitzsch raised the gun to eye level and examined the lock.

Slowly he approached the "Black Wall." That is what this part of the wall was called. It was covered with fiberboard, and the executions were carried out in front of it.

The next moment, we saw Bronek. He brought in a naked elderly man whose hands were behind his back, bound together with wire. In front of the "Black Wall," they stopped. Bronek departed. Palitzsch pushed the elderly man further ahead and placed him with his face to the wall. At the same time, Palitzsch lifted the gun to the level of his neck and pulled the trigger. A shot and the man took half a step forward, and then fell facedown onto the sandy ground. Blood gushed from the back of his head. . . .

Hauptscharführer Palitzsch stepped carefully aside, and Entreß appeared on the scene.

He bent down to the one lying on the ground, pulling his hair and lifting his head in order to determine the reaction of the pupils; he then felt his pulse and said loudly to Palitzsch:

"Okay!"

Palitzsch motioned with his hand. The prisoners, whom Hans had been calling out of the washroom shortly earlier, came running out of the Block. They carried a long box, which was used for the transport of corpses. They threw the old man into that box. Bronek started to throw sand over the ground, which was soaked with blood. The sand was from the bucket which he had brought from the Block.

After two minutes, during which time the SS men were smoking their cigarettes, the traces of the execution were obliterated.

Palitzsch again approached the "Black Wall."

Wacek and the three prisoners returned to the Block and, after a while, Bronek appeared again.

This time he led a woman. She was a somewhat elderly person with grey hair. She was trembling, and she looked around with fearful eyes. She was only wearing an undershirt, which reached down to her knees. . . . Her hands were similarly bound behind her back with wire. . . .

In front of the "Black Wall," they stopped. Bronek left, and Palitzsch placed his victim with her back turned towards him and lifted the gun.

A shot . . . A scream . . . The woman took a half turn on her right foot and fell down.

Again Entreß. A short examination. Then Wacek and his comrades completed their tasks, and a new corpse covered the first one already in the box.

This time the box was carried away.

Bronek leveled off the sand, which was soaked with blood. He brought new sand, sprinkled it over the ground, and then fetched a new victim.

This was a young woman of about twenty-eight years of age. She only wore panties. She walked about slowly and crimsoned with shame; she lowered her head as if thus trying to cover her breasts and shield them from the eyes of the men.

The SS men were prying at her curiously.

The SS physician took off his glasses, wiped them clumsily with a handkerchief, and put them back on. He stretched his head forward in order to see better.

And again Palitzsch, again a new shot . . . He did not aim well enough; therefore, the woman was still standing. She stood on the spot, and blood was pouring from the back of her head. She lifted her head a bit higher and opened her eyes widely; her tongue pushed forward a bit from her opened mouth. . . .

A scream penetrated the heavens . . . long, monotonously, horribly. . . . All that lasted for about a second, which, however, seemed like eternity.

Palitzsch threw away his gun and reached for his pistol. Its oxidized steel flared up in the sun. The second shot was better targeted; the woman fell down. . . . Her screaming fell into silence. However, *SS–Hauptscharführer* Palitzsch still did not trust his revolver bullet. He bent down to the one lying on the ground, and from a ten-centimeter distance, he shot again, twice.

After that he got up, he wiped his face with his hand . . . Silence . . . The rest of the SS men stood there motionlessly, and the SS physician was suddenly in no hurry with the pronouncement of her death.

That lasted for about a minute.

Finally Palitzsch said loudly, "*SS-Obersturmführer* Entreß . . . please determine the death!" His voice sounded hard, like metal, admonishing, like a rebuke.

After this execution, there was a pause. The uniformed men stood closely together, but they did not speak a word. Palitzsch smoked a cigarette and puffed curls into the air . . . calmly, as if nothing had happened.

Bronek, very pale, nervously leveled the ground. He closed his eyes repeatedly and was breathing heavily.

Palitzsch noticed that.

"What? Tell me, are you not well?" he called out to him.

Bronek took off his cap, as was required by camp protocol during a talk with an SS man, and replied:

"Everything is okay, *Herr Haupscharführer*. I am fine."

"Then you are lucky!"

The prisoners returned with the box into which the bloody corpse of the woman disappeared. The lid was closed, and the box was placed aside.

Gerlach asked if the "work" could proceed. . . . Palitzsch extinguished his cigarette butt with his boot, and:

"The next," he muttered.

And again Bronek appeared. Next to him was a little girl about eight to nine years old. Naked. Her large, light-blue eyes looked inquisitively but with fear around her surroundings. Her hands were, like those of all the others, bound together with wire.

Even now, I still hear her asking with a shaking voice:

"What is going to happen? Where is Mama? Who are these gentlemen?"

Bronek held the girl by her arm and said nothing. He is blinking with his eyes uninterruptedly, and he presses his lips together.

The little girl continues to ask questions, but she is already standing too far away from our window, and I can no longer understand the meaning of her words.

The SS men are silent, staring at the ground. Fritzsch is playing nervously with his fingers. Entreß is carefully cleaning his glasses. This time, however, he does not put them on.

Palitzsch smiled at the girl. He is saying something and is leading her by her arm to the "Black Wall."

I feel a lump in my throat, my heart is pounding loudly . . . I cling desperately to the windowsill.

Roman, prisoner no. 6576, is weeping silently. . . . He is a man of large, athletic stature. Now he appears very small, as if he had shriveled up, his head hanging low.

"Bandits . . . Bandits . . .," he is continually repeating. "What has this child done to them? . . . Bandits, Bandits . . .!"

Palitzsch stops. He moves the girl forward, but he is holding her arm with his left hand.

With his right hand he is lifting the gun.

I cannot watch this any longer and move to the other corner of the washroom.

Romek remains at the window.

"I have to stay here . . . I must see it . . . Sometime I will have to tell this to the world. . . . Bandits!"

A shot is falling.

Quickly, I return to the window.

The small body is lying on the yellow, sandy ground. Her hair is forming a strange harmony with the color of the sand. The blood similarly . . . Palitzsch shows great interest in his gun. He takes out the lock and manipulates around the casing. His movements are balanced; he is very calm. "Wilhelm Tell!" He demonstrates how controlled and hard one ought to be! He is looking down with contempt at his comrades. "Weaklings!" he must certainly be thinking. He pretends to be very indifferent although today marked his anniversary. Just this moment he had executed the thousandth human being. That indeed is an "achievement" for just one year!

Now he is looking at the rest of the SS men and is laughing:

"I invite you all to a celebration today. It is an anniversary celebration. The little person whom I have just now executed in Auschwitz for the Führer has been the thousandth. I presume you are coming?"

His voice is clearly ironic.

Fritzsch is getting up:

"Your private matters, I ask you, to discuss after duty, *Hauptscharfüher*!"

Palitzsch is controlling himself: "Yes, *Hauptsturmführer*!" Standing at attention, he is loudly clicking his heels and motions to Gerlach.

Wacek and the others place the dead body in the box. Bronek is not with them. I learned later that he had suffered a nervous breakdown and had attempted to hang himself in the Bunker. At the last moment, however, Hans had rescued him.

All this transpired within seconds. Wacek had already learned of Bronek's intentions, and, therefore, he himself levels the sandy ground. Of course, Palitzsch is noticing that.

"Where is the boilerman?"

Wacek is not *Stubenältester* in the SK without reason. He is quickly finding a proper response:

"Just a while ago, he slipped on the stairs of the bunker and sprained his leg. He is now resting in the barrack room. After work, he will be carried to the hospital building." Without faltering, he is downrightly lying.

"Is that right?" Palitzsch's eyes look at him with distrust.

"Yes, that is true!" Wacek again replied.

Palitzsch turns to Gerlach. He does not know that Gerlach, along with Wacek, is drunk every day. Together they kill; together they rape the women in detention, although one wears the uniform of an SS man and the other the jacket of a prisoner.

"That is true, *Hauptscharführer*!" Gerlach confirms.

"Okay. The next."

The next does not walk; he is carried.

He really cannot walk yet because only eleven weeks have passed in his life. Gerlach carries him in his arms. The little boy is crying terribly. His little body is entirely pink. The small head covered with fine hair is not much larger than Gerlach's fist.

"This is the last one, *Hauptscharführer*!" Gerlach reports, holding the child in front of him.

Palitzsch looked at his comrades. Their silence is irritating him. For a while he seems to reflect, and then he puts away his gun.

"A bullet is too good for something like this," he is saying loudly, while looking at the SS men.

He reaches for the baby whom Gerlach is handing to him. Both of its little legs find enough space in his fist. One can hear a weak cry from the small child.

Palitzsch reaches back and is hitting the baby with its head against the Wall. Immediately the crying subsides; a spot remains on the wall while Palitzsch is throwing the little dead body to the ground.

"Please determine the death, *Hauptsturmführer*!" he screamed with an unnatural voice.

Fritzsch and the other SS men turn around and make their way to the gate. Meanwhile, Entreß is responding to Palitzsch:

"Death has certainly occurred. With your routine any uncertainty is out of the question." Entreß is pale and his lips are quivering. His aesthetic senses were obviously violated. He himself does only "clean work." He only decides who should die by way of injection or the gas chamber.

Palitzsch remains with Gerlach in the square. He is angry. "Did you hear the sensitive gentleman? Dr. Entreß was embarrassed. He does not like this dirty work. I have killed a thousand human beings, and I am proud of it. If I would get the order, I would execute one hundred thousand . . . even a Million, and I would always be proud of it. Herr Entreß determines with each selection a hundred, even a thousand, who should die, and he is ashamed to be brave. Pfui!" He spat on the ground and walked through the gate, leaning on his gun.

Gerlach followed him before long.

The little body, which was rolled together, was still lying on the yellow sand. Wacek and Hans walked around it while cleaning the square.

In the washroom it was quiet. Roman stopped crying. He looked into the square and was unable to remove his eyes from the Black Wall. Desperately, he pressed his lips together; he was breathing fast. I touch his arm:

"Roman!"

His raised his head, as if just awakening.

"What do you want?"

"Come up here!"

Suddenly he cast one more glance through the window, pushed me aside, and ran to the door.

I ran after him.

Roman ran quickly to the little body and lifted it carefully with both hands.

I stood as if nailed to the ground and was unable to go one step further.

For a little while, Roman looked at the child, and then he went to the box and placed the small body next to the girl, on the bloodstained breasts of the young woman, the mother of the two children.

These were the family members of prisoner Johann Przywara from Zamosc, who had escaped a few days ago.

According to the ordinance of *SS-Reichsführer* Himmler, they were exterminated.

6

One day a transport arrived from Cracow, all of which was assigned to the Punishment Company (SK). It consisted of several Poles and about twenty Jews. During the evening roll call, *Blockführer* Gerlach conducted, as usual, the inspection of the new arrivals. For a moment, he stopped in front of the tall figure of an elderly man who clearly stood out from the rest.

"What is your profession?" he asked.

"I am a priest."

"Aha!" The SS man's eyes flared up bestially. "Perhaps you came here trying to correct our ways, didn't you?"

The priest, Karczmarczek from the vicinity of Cracow, did not answer. He looked steadily into Gerlach's eyes. In his looks there was something self-confident, something steadfast.

"We shall soon find out whether or not you have a heart!" the *Blockführer* suddenly said. He went a few meters further, to where the Jews were standing. He dragged the first one out of line and took him to Karczmarczek. "Do you see this dog?"

The priest did not answer him this time either.

"That is a Jew." the SS man continued. "They have crucified your Christ; now you have an opportunity to pay them back." He gave the priest his bullwhip. "Take that and belt him twenty-five."

The priest Karczmarczek straightened up even higher. Without a word, he looked at his feet, ignoring the outstretched hand with the bullwhip.

Blood rushed into Gerlach's face.

"What, you dare not to carry out my order?" There was a sudden motion of the hand, and the bullwhip hit the face of the priest. "You stupid dog, perhaps you want to become a saint. I will make that easier for you. . . ." This time he turned to the Jew, whose entire body was trembling. "Do you know how long a Jew will be alive here?"

Scared to death, the Jew shook his head.

"You don't know, isn't that true? At the most, ten days. But I like you. I shall give you a double ration of food. I will also make you a *Stubendienst*. Do you understand?"

The Jew was trembling with fear and nodded. "Yes, Sir!" "As *Stubendienst*, you must above all be obedient. You will have to carry out every order. Do you understand?"

"Yes, Sir!"

Gerlach's face expressed a restrained satanic grin. For a moment, he looked silently at the prisoner, and then he said: "Now let us try to find out whether you are suitable for duty as a *Stubendienst*. Here!" He handed him the bullwhip.

The trembling fingers of the Jew desperately grasped the handle of the whip. Gerlach was beaming.

"Yes, excellent! You will certainly survive the camp. Do you see this old man?" He pointed to Karczmarczek.

A nodding.

"Come here!" This time the order was directed to the priest, who stepped slowly out of the line.

"Bend down!" was the next order.

Karczmarczek was bending down.

"Give him twenty-five!" He gave the order with a raised voice.

And now something entirely unexpected happened. The small, until now trembling, figure of Symcha Szmedras, the little tailor from Podgorze, began to rise up; he seemed to grow and appeared to expand into gigantic dimensions. A strangely solemn silence settled over the breathlessly waiting line of the Punishment Company (SK). . . .

The little Jew's arms stretched out as if trying to stand at attention. His consumptive chest began to pant and rise. His eyes, which until now had expressed a terrible fear, suddenly began to glow. . . .

"Did you hear me? You are to smack him twenty-five times!" Gerlach repeated his order.

Drops of sweat resembling silver pearls appeared on Szmedras's forehead. For a while, he continued to look undecidedly down at his feet. Then he raised his head powerfully and spoke with a faintly trembling voice:

"I shall not beat him!"

We held our breath. The sight of Szmedras, who stood with a lifted head and radiant eyes in front of the gigantic Gerlach, gave a supernatural impression.

For moments, there was silence, filled with horrible anticipation. Gerlach's face began to crimson, as if at any moment blood would rush out of his veins. His eyes were squeezed together as if in a seizure. He walked one step towards the Jew. "What?" In this question his entire rabid madness exploded. "You are not going to beat him? You? You stupid Jewish dog, you refuse to carry out my order?" His fist, not much smaller than Szmedras's head, hit the Jew with a terrible blow.

Szmedras fell to the floor as if struck by lightning. In the next moment, the studded boots of the SS man hit the stomach of the one lying on the floor. A heart-piercing scream roared out. Szmedras doubled up with pain. The next kick was aimed at the area of the kidneys. Again a scream . . . One simply could not take it. *SS-Rottenführer* Gerlach was hacking and beating simultaneously. One had the impression that hacking and beating were not enough for him, that he would have loved to tear him into pieces. . . . The reverberations of the blows and Gerlach's heavy breathing pierced through the ghastly silence. Symcha Szmedras was no longer screaming. . . .

Finally, Gerlach stopped. With his enormous, overblown claws, he stood still for a while over the one lying on the ground; then he wiped away his sweat with a handkerchief.

And just then, another unexpected incident occurred. The priest Karczmarczek, who until now had remained standing to the side, moved suddenly. With slow, dignified steps, he walked toward the Jew lying on the floor and made the sign of the cross over him. The silence became unbearable. Each of us felt a choking lump in the throat.

The tall figure of the priest, his proudly raised head, which was circled with a ring of silver hair as if with a halo, his lips moving in prayer, made an indescribable impression on us. Even *Kapo* Johny moved his head restlessly, blinked a few times, and remained silent.

Gerlach looked upon all this with amazement. One could see that he had not yet decided how he should proceed further. For a moment something like fear seemed to struggle in his face with his ever-increasing rage. For a short span of time, we even had the impression that he intended to turn around and walk away.

But he probably remembered the motto of the SS: "Our honor is called loyalty. . . ."

And he remained "loyal." He ran to the priest, who was still kneeling, and, on his way, he seized a heavy club from the hand of a *Vorarbeiter*.

"You greedy dog! You want to conduct a prayer service here!" The priest continued to pray. He did not seem to hear the raving mad *Blockführer* or to see the club raised above his head.

Even when he was already lying on the floor, blood pouring out of his mouth from the blows and kicks, we heard a faint "God, have mercy on the sinful soul! . . ."

And then a long silence prevailed. Gerlach disappeared almost unnoticed. The *Blockälteste* Hans ordered us to step aside, and *Kapo* Johny gave orders to the *Stubenältesten* in a grumpy voice.

"Carry the two into the washroom. And you may wash them a bit. . . ." Embarrassed, he looked to the ground and said to himself, "Both of them had a heart, one really has to grant them that. . . ."

Then he went with heavy steps to the barrack room.

When the pallbearers from the hospital barracks carried the dead ones out of the washroom in the evening, almost the entire SK gathered in the square. Even Reinhold and similar people were sneaking around the gate.

When the pallbearers appeared on the stairs with the closed box, all, as if on command, took off their caps and stood at attention. In the history of the SK, this was perhaps the only public tribute which was extended to murdered prisoners.

Until the gong sounded, there was a solemn silence in all barrack rooms. Nobody screamed and even the VIPs of the camp seemed to have lost their importance and dreadfulness this evening.

When the gong resounded, even Komarnicki himself, said only, "Go to bed, it is already late" instead of screaming, as he usually did.

The lights went out just as a heavy thunderstorm was approaching outside.

Here and there, one could hear the whispering of prayers. And, perhaps for the first time in the history of the Punishment Company (SK), no one was beaten for his prayer.

From the corner of the hall which was occupied by the *Kapos*, one could soon hear snoring. I had, however, the impression that it all sounded much too noisy and artificial. . . .

7

On this day of September, after our work was done, we were led not back to our Block 11 but instead to the ground of the still incomplete Block 5. The *Blockältesten* informed us that the purpose for this unreasonable re-quartering was the disinfection of the old Block.

Since the fifth Block was located in the area of the general camp, this requartering gave cause for general joy. Here we were protected from roll calls by the *Kapos*. Furthermore, the absence of the isolation wall gave our comrades from the general camp the opportunity, to provide us with some food. However, after a quiet roll call, the *Kapos*, the *Stubenältesten*, and the *Vorarbeiter* usually formed a line which separated our block from the rest of the Camp. Despite that, many comrades received quite a decent amount of "food waste". . . . The next day, the news reached us that an entire transport of Russian prisoners of war had been driven into Block 11. This event was interpreted in different ways. Some argued that the Punishment Company (SK) was to be entirely dissolved; others knew from "reliable sources" that the Russians would be executed on our Block; still others had important expressions on their faces implying that they knew much more but could not say anything. One thing, however, was certain; today we could not yet return to the "11".

On the morning of the third day, before our march to work, *Stubendienst* Wacek, with a pompous expression on his face, ordered those prisoners who were well built and could still be designated as strong to step forward. I belonged to the twenty who were chosen. The Company marched away to work, but we remained on the Block.

Not one of us knew what this was all about. After half an hour, Wacek returned.

"Listen! You have remained in the camp and you will receive an extra helping at the meals. However, you have to start immediately with "special work"! At the same time, you will also be able to take something for yourselves, but you will have to keep your mouths shut. Understood?"

Although no one had understood him, we nevertheless answered in unison, "Yes, Sir!"

During the next quarter of an hour, we waited in line until Gerlach came. He scrutinized us meticulously, nodded and turned to us with a few unclear sentences, just as Wacek had already done:

"In a few minutes you will begin with 'confidential work.' If any one of you will give away even one word about what you will be seeing,"—at that point Gerlach made a significant gesture with his hand around his throat—"kaput! . . . A small heap of ashes in the crematory! You will get plenty to eat. . . . Understood?"

Again we did not understand a thing. One thing, however, became clear to us: the work for which we were designated could cost us our heads. That much we all understood. Nevertheless, the promise that we would get plenty to eat had a comforting effect. That was important.

After a few minutes, we walked in double line through the gate of the main Block 11.

In the square were present: the representative of *Lagerführer* Fritzsch, *SS-Obersturmführer* Mayer, the *Rapportführer* of the camp, *SS-Hauptscharführer* Palitzsch, the camp physician, *SS-Obersturmführer* Entreß, *SS-Oberscharführer* Klehr, *SS-Unterscharführer* Stark, *Kriminalassistent* Woznica of the local political section, and our two *Blockführer* Gerlach and Edelhardt.

Wacek gave the prescribed order "Caps off!" and reported to Mayer, "Twenty prisoners have reported to work."

He exchanged a few words with the *Rapportführer*. After that he said something to Wacek.

The *Stubenälteste* shouted, "Yes, Sir!" and turned toward us. "Each of you will receive a gas mask. Fit it on tightly so that the others will not have to be called to carry you out. Understood?"

"Yes, Sir!"

At the wall there was a large box with gas masks. They were quickly distributed among us.

After only three minutes, we were ready, donned with gas masks. *SS-Oberscharführer* Klehr made sure that everyone's gas mask was fitted tightly.

All that happened so fast that we had no time to collect our thoughts. We looked at each other quietly without understanding anything about all that was happening.

Our "uniformed men" also put on gas masks. Wacek and the *Bunkerkapo*, Kurt Pennewitz, ran nervously back and forth to the Block several times, spoke there with Palitzsch, who unwillingly shook his head, and then both of them ran back, and thus it continued, back and forth.

Finally, all the SS men pulled their pistols. The chromed barrel of a submachine gun flashed with hostility in Palitzch's hand.

"They want to execute us!" was our first thought. Our throats begin to tighten, and our eyelids begin to burn. The air in the mask is thick; it is difficult to inhale.

Instinctively, we move closer together. Someone tries to pull down the mask. For that he receives a blow to his neck with the handle of a pistol; he is falling to the ground. The seconds move terribly slowly.

They don't shoot! Not yet . . .

Perhaps they really will not execute us?

This new thought calms me down, and I look around. The SS men hold the pistols ready to fire; however, they do not shoot.

Palitzsch motions to Wacek.

"Ready! Begin!"

The *Stubenälteste* comes running toward us.

"Do not be afraid; follow!" He turns toward the Block. We run after him and Palitzsch, Stark, and some other SS men follow us. I am near the end of our group. The barrel of a "shooting iron" of the person behind me touches my back. I force myself forward and walk right behind Wacek.

He is walking down the stairs. For a moment we stop . . . all . . . Bunker!. . . The SS men, however, don't give us any time to think. At the end of the group, someone is already down.

"Go on! Go on!"

Wacek is stopping at the door of the Bunker. In his right hand, he is carrying an axe. He is putting it into his left hand, and with his right hand he reaches for a key in his pocket.

It is obvious that he cannot find the key hole because it is lasting for a few minutes. The voice of Palitzsch yells from the end of the group, "Faster!"

Finally he got it. The key turns in the lock. Wacek grasps for the door handle. Instinctively, I hold my breadth. I moisten my lips, which in the meantime have become very dry. What's going to happen now? . . .

Wacek is walking back. He takes the axe into his hand again.

What does all this mean?

What is the purpose of the axe here?

Why is he afraid?

He is grasping the door handle a second time, this time with his left hand. The right hand, in which he is holding the axe, he is lifting up, as if ready to deal a terrible blow.

I begin to freeze, and suddenly I am seized by fear. That is a different kind of fear than the one which I experienced previously. Now I am not afraid for myself. No, but I am panic-stricken with fear of this door. My heart is pounding strongly. Beneath the rubber bands of the gas mask, I clearly feel every beat of my pulse.

Wacek pushes down the door handle while he is moving a meter backwards and forcefully pulling open the door.

The door opens, and at that moment I feel how my shorn hair is standing up.

About a meter in front of me, there are upright-standing human beings! Crowded together, somehow terribly twisted, with terribly protruding eyes, scratched, besmeared with blood, motionlessly . . .

Those who had been leaning on the door tilted, strangely stiff, fall upon us and bounce hard, facedown, onto the stony floor, close to our feet. Corpses . . . very stiffly standing corpses . . . They fill the entire corridor of the Bunker. However, they are so closely crowded together that they cannot really fall down.

For a moment, I feel nauseated.

Wacek's voice is bringing me back to my senses.

"Okay!" Carry them out!"...

Now I am thinking clearly again, and I understand everything.

The corpses wore the uniforms of the Red Army. It must certainly be that transport that we talked about yesterday while at work. They were all driven into the Bunker, and there they were gassed. Therefore, we had to put on gas masks. That riddle has now been solved!

Wacek takes the first corpse under his arms and is handing it on to us.

"That is what it is!" I am now thinking. "It will now be our work to carry the gassed ones out of the Bunker."

"Line up!" Wacek is screaming again. "Form a chain!"

"The chain" was usually a means which could help one quickly pass on bricks when unloading a railroad truck. However, it never occurred to me during the unloading of bricks that one could "load" human beings in a similar way.

We worked late into the night.

After we had emptied the Bunker, we still had to undress the dead ones and put their clothing into a special heap. The next day, they would wander into the "dressing room" to increase its stock.

We counted 1473 Russian uniforms and more than 190 pieces of camp clothing. The latter belonged to the sick ones from the hospital whom *SS-Obersturmführer* Entreß had designated as "unfit for work." On this occasion, they had been gassed together with the Russian prisoners of war. . . .

After our "work" was done, the twenty of us received a fifty-liter kettle full of soup; in addition, each of us received half a loaf of bread.

The entire kettle was returned to the Block—almost untouched.

This was the first time that gas was used in Auschwitz as a means of liquidating the prisoners.

8

The author is dedicating this chapter to the following uncompromising fighters for human rights in concentration camps (KZ): Dr. Alex Cepicka, Josef Cyrankiewicz, and Hermann Langbein.

AT THE BEGINNING OF autumn, the vacant position of the *Oberkapo* was filled. The position of the continually drunken Adolf, who died after drinking a bottle of methanol, was taken by Teo Brüning from Essen. His background was very controversial and, indeed, an entire garland of legends was formed around his person. Several prisoners asserted that he had been a bigwig in the Party, who, it was told, had been actively involved against Hitler in the underground movement after he had learned the "true values" of the ideology of National Socialism. Others thought he might have been a cousin of the former Imperial Chancellor, and still others had information they obtained from a "reliable source" that Teo had not so long ago worn the uniform of a high-ranking army officer.

Whose assertions were correct, I did not know. It remained, however, a fact that from the first day onward Teo enjoyed special consideration in the camp. He was not required to shave his head, he received his meals from the SS kitchen, and one could notice that wherever he went, the SS men had special instructions regarding him. Teo's appearance stood in full contrast to that of the other *Kapos*. He was of tall stature with intelligent facial expressions; a sophisticated, high forehead; and calm, dark eyes.

After the general "roll call" for work, he moved to the head of the Punishment Company (SK) and, as usual, we marched to the gravel pit. After having arrived there, Teo gave his first order according to the work allocations. All clubs of every *Kapo* and *Vorarbeiter* must be turned in at the hut.

The present *Kommandoführer* did not trust his eyes.

"What does that mean?"

Teo took off his cap and said:

"A cane serves the purpose of support, *Kommandoführer*. Our functional prisoners look quite healthy."

The SS man's jaw dropped. For a while he looked at Teo as if he was insane, and finally he blew his top:

"And with what are they supposed to beat?"

"The point is, they will not beat anyone! Beating reduces work efficiency, and I have orders from the *Arbeitsdienstführer* to increase the results of the work performance."

"You must be crazy? This gang is not going to work at all without a beating."

"That is going to be seen in the future." Teo cast a glance at the line of the SK and blinked.

"May I send the people to work now?"

The SS man crimsoned with rage.

"Nonsense!" he shouted. "The *Kapos* will have to have clubs. I give orders here!"

Teo clicked his heals. "You keep watch over us, *Kommandoführer*. It is your duty to place the guards and to see to it that no one escapes. I, on the other hand, take care of the work allocation and control its performance." He said it calmly but with a decisive tone.

The SS man looked at Teo and was speechless. "What are you really thinking? You forget that you too are a prisoner just as anyone else," he said, pointing toward us, "and you can easily lose the armband of *Oberkapo* along with your head."

"I have never forgotten that I am a prisoner, and at the same time, I will not forget that you are an SS man. I know that independently of losing my armband, I may lose my head. I counted on it since that day when I put on my prisoner jacket. By the way, *Kommandoführer*,"—he looked at his watch—"we are already talking for eight minutes; two- hundred-and-fifty prisoners are standing idly during that time, eight times two-hundred-and-fifty makes 2, 000 minutes, which means thirty-three and three tenths of working hours which the state has lost, only because you were talking with me; because we can on the average load ten sand trucks with gravel, we lost about three hundred trucks of gravel which are desperately needed for the construction of factory plants. Are you trying to sabotage this work any longer?" Teo spoke the last words in a raised voice while looking the *Kommandoführer* straight in the eye.

This time, the SS man did not say a word. He waved his hand and went to his hut.

Teo returned to us.

"Did everyone hear that? Get on with your work!"

On this morning, more gravel was loaded than on any other day during the entire shift.

After lunch, a new incident occurred in which Teo completely conquered the prisoners' hearts.

Karl Dachdecker, the most feared *Kapo* of the SK, caught a young lad smoking a cigarette in the latrine.

"You dirty dog!" Karl's fist landed in the young prisoner's stomach area. "You have perhaps developed a taste for smoking, huh? What's the matter with you, you pig!"

The screams of the beaten one lured Teo to the spot. He ran quickly to the latrine and pulled the furious Dachdecker away from his victim

"I have announced today that beating is forbidden!"

"You can kick me somewhere!" Karl was unable to control himself and acted as if he were crazy. "I am going to strike this dog dead. And you," he said, turning to Teo, "you better watch out so that you will not get hurt either." "You Polish pig!" He again turned to the young lad.

Teo immediately began to take revenge. Quickly his fist reached Karl's jar bone, while his left hand hit his stomach area. The heavy Karl tumbled a few meters and hit the wall of the latrine. But he soon got a hold of himself and proceeded with a counterattack.

However, Teo was faster. With a professional boxer's technique, he kept Karl at an appropriate distance, whereby he gave him a series of well-aimed hooks to the chin.

Karl was lying motionlessly on the ground, screaming.

"And now, after I have given you a deserving response to your threats and your general mean disposition towards me, I am still going to speak for this boy. You called him, 'Polish pig,' did you not?"

Karl, lying on the floor, nodded obediently.

"Yes, however, I am really a German of the Reich," he said apologetically.

"No, dear, you are a bandit, and as such you were incarcerated in jail, and later you came into the camp. Your own state, your own nation, has excluded you from the national community, which means you are a 'bad'

German of the Third Reich. The reason why this boy, however, came into the camp is because of his nation; he was a good person, a good Pole. And there, we Germans have incarcerated him as a political prisoner in this camp and you call him 'pig,'"—he shook his head—"you should be ashamed of yourself, Karl." Now he helped him to get up and brushed him off while he continued his conversation. "You see, Karl, we were all incarcerated here in the Concentration Camp (KZ) by our enemies. Those who incarcerated me and our German comrades have also incarcerated our comrades of other nations: Poles, Russians, Jews, Frenchmen, Czechs, etc. We are all in the same situation. And as for us, for the others, too, mothers, wives, and children wait at home. We all really have the same fate. Behind the barbed wires, we all form a closely knit and closed community, and some time we all want to have freedom, you, I, and many others. But we can only become free if we stick together as a great family." Teo raised his head even higher: "We have to help each other. We must show the SS men through our behavior that the national differences, in contrast to their ideology, is a lot of nonsense, that people of different nations can be brothers and live fraternally. Do you understand that?" He looked questioningly at Karl.

The latter looked at him with distrust.

"Tell me, do you understand that?" Teo repeated his question.

"Are you by any chance a Biblical scholar?" Dachdecker countered with another question.

Teo lowered his head.

"No. I am only a human being."

"May I depart now? "Karl asked suddenly.

"Go ahead!"

Dachdecker went away, slowly. Immediately his "comrades" surrounded him.

"What did he want from you? What was happening there? Did he beat you?"

"A crazy dog!" Karl responded. "He tried to convert me to love the Jews, Poles, Russians, and other such trash nations. We should establish a family . . . ha, ha, ha!"

Karl started laughing heartily about this thought. "A strange fool," he added.

"Well, that is really something!" Reinhold was similarly outraged.

"I am of the opinion that you should report this immediately to the *Kommandoführer*."

Karl's finger tipped his own head.

"That, by the way, is a good idea. It might thus be possible to get rid of this crazy guy. If he were to be deprived of his *Oberkapo* armband, then I would like to get him into my pit."

Karl smiled about his idea.

"Let's go!"

They went to the hut. Shortly thereafter, one could hear a calling:

"*Oberkapo* to the *Kommandoführer*!"

However, in the meantime, Teo was informed about the intentions of the henchmen by other prisoners. He straightened out his garb, placed his cap properly, and shook the hands of those standing close to him.

"You don't have to worry about me! Nothing will happen to me. I have a good backing."

After a while, he returned, content and smiling. We immediately surrounded him. "Well, how was it?"

"Well, I told you already that nothing would happen to me. Everything is Okay!"

Since this incident, there was an entirely different atmosphere in the Punishment Company (SK). Teo's influence was really great. The beating ceased almost entirely, and the roll calls were shorter than before. After our work was done, we indeed had free time.

And the most important thing: The food rations were honestly distributed. Teo saw everything and was everywhere. The other *Kapos* accepted it and no longer opposed him openly. In their dark souls, however, they vowed revenge.

This idyll lasted several weeks until Teo became ill one day and had to be carried to the hospital barracks.

The command was overtaken by *Kapo* Johny.

From this moment onwards, the old conditions returned to the SK.

9

At the beginning of November, our workplace changed. We no longer worked in the gravel pit but instead had to dig trenches for potatoes and beets. Because our workplace was located several kilometers away from the camp, our superiors thought that we could not have our lunch there, and therefore they changed the procedure by packing our evening rations into boxes which were divided among us during lunchtime. We would therefore receive our soup in the evening. This actually insignificant change provided our *Kapos* and *Vorarbeiter* with the opportunity for "new feats." The distribution of bread was, of course, in their hands. And for bread one could buy almost anything in the camp: cigarettes, fat soup and even brandy.

They began to harass us. A few "work overseers" were chosen, who had to walk up and down between the groups of the working prisoners. On the basis of their own discretion, they would write down the numbers of those who were apparently lazy at work. The bearers of these numbers were called out before the distribution of bread and were placed in one group together. They were informed that as a penalty they were to be deprived of their food rations. The number of those who were punished daily in this manner was always more than fifty. The daily victims were added to that, so that the daily "profit" from bread rations amounted to about eighty.

One of the new arrivals, who was deprived of almost his entire daily ration in this way, went, against our advice, with a complaint to the *Kommandoführer. SS-Oberscharführer* Edelhardt considered his complaint an attempted mutiny, and, as a deterrent, he shot him in front of the entire company. After this day, all of those who were punished were "very content."

We now had to work much faster than we were already used to working. In order to make the supervision easier, we were divided into smaller groups of ten men. Each group was headed by a *Vorarbeiter*. Each prisoner was expected to lift out about twenty cubic meters of trenches daily. One could not accomplish that load of work, not even with the exertion of all of one's energies. The reason for this was that during our previous long stay in the camp, all of us were in such bad shape that at times we could hold a shovel in our hands only with great exertion. Some of us collapsed at that time, even without having been beaten. To make matters worse, the autumn of this year was exceptionally cold. At the beginning of October, we already had daily frost. Coats, socks, gloves or hats were out of the question. Our entire clothing consisted of light underwear and not much heavier overalls; these were an inheritance from the Russian prisoners of war, who had been gassed. The luckier ones of us had boots with wooden soles on their feet. The rest, about eighty per cent, were walking in wooden clogs. During work, they were all shaking and clattering with their teeth because of the cold. The *Kommandoführer*, however, gave "ingenious" advice regarding this situation. Early in the morning, he ordered us to take off our jackets. "And if you should be freezing," he added smilingly, "then just work faster!"

One day after this order about ten men became ill with pneumonia.

After about two weeks, I was totally exhausted. In the morning, I crawled out of my bed with difficulty. Since five days earlier they had lifted the ban on the Punishment Company (SK) making use of the quarters for the sick, I reported to the *Stubendienst* that I was ill. He examined me quite thoroughly, checked my throat and said:

"We shall see. Get in line for the inspection of the sick!"

In the line for the "sick," there were already about twenty prisoners. After the company had marched to work, the *Blockälteste* appeared, accompanied by Gerlach.

The inspection did not last very long. While *Blockführer* Gerlach was walking along our line, he asked everyone:

"What?"

And before the one who was being questioned could answer, he was hit with a blow to the stomach. If, as a result, he should fall to the ground, the *Blockälteste* would continue to work him over; if he did not fall down, he was left alone. I victoriously survived this strange inspection and marched, after half an hour, together with an additional nine "chosen ones," to Block 28. The outpatient section was located there. First, we were examined by Dr. Rudolf Diem, a physician, who was a prisoner himself and bore the number 10022. One did not have to tell him too much. The dark dot, the badge of the SK, sufficed to be considered eligible for the hospital barracks. However, Dr. Diem's opinion was not sufficient. One had to be subjected to another examination, which was conducted by SS physician, *Obersturmführer,* Entreß. In case of his absence, *Sanitätsunteroffizier* of the camp, *SS-Oberscharführer* Klehr, a butcher from Breslau, conducted the examination instead.

We were all led into the "washroom," which had a concrete floor, wet walls and, by order of the SS, permanently opened windows.

"Take off your clothes!"

The barbers, also prisoners, cut the hair: on the head, under the armpits, and on the lower abdomen. The dull hair clippers rip apart, but that does not bother anyone. If only the hair would be gone already!

After the hair is cut, a bath follows. Ice cold water is streaming from two showers. There is no trace of any soap.

With clattering teeth, we have to stand in the corner and wait. Finally the medical attendant for the prisoners is leading us into hall number 7. Again we have to wait! The bodies are steaming because of the cold. The windows are always open. Each time the door is opened, an ice cold draft is blowing through the room. The group of naked and shivering prisoners presses together. Perhaps we will be able to warm each other. . . . One of the patients, who has diarrhea, is leaning against the wall, turning pale. Desperately he pushes together his legs, which resemble stilts and are covered with yellow, wrinkled skin. On that part where his buttocks ought to be, there are only two protruding bones, and immediately below, there is a horrible hole. . . . It is running down his legs . . . the excretions smell especially revolting. . . . The medical attendant for the prisoners is bringing him a stool from somewhere. He is carefully cleaning him up with cellulose and is setting him down. A while later, it is running down the stool.

Within the crowded group on the wall, there are others. The air is unbearable.

Close to me, there stands a prisoner with a strong inflammation on his right foot. A yellow, strong-smelling discharge of pus is running out of his five-centimeter-wide wound. I am getting nauseated. . . .

A sick person with typhoid fever is beginning to get delirious. He is screaming continually, while looking toward the door, "Mama! Mama! Mama!"

The medical attendants for the prisoners, who are running between us with cellulose in their hands, attempt to pacify him. The delirious prisoner is resisting them. He pushes two other patients. They fall to the ground and scream terribly.

After short intervals a new "transport" of freshly bathed prisoners arrives. Altogether we are already fifty men. A few of them are already lying on the floor and are moaning softly. That is lasting for about an hour.

Around nine o'clock, Georg, the supervisor of the registration room, prisoner number 616, dashes into the hall:

"The camp physician! Line up!"

Those who are sick with diarrhea are again cleaned up. Georg admonishes them, "And don't shit by accident on the *SS-Obersturmführer*!"

Finally the line is ready, and the command is falling. "March!" . . . Corridor . . . the wet soles of the feet hurt like scalded wounds as soon as they touch the wet floor. The outpatient section is located at the first door to the right.

The room is opulent with cleanliness for the reception of the camp physician. Cabinets, walls, windows, everything is sparkling so that one can see his reflection in them. The windows are now closed because *Herr SS-Obersturmführer* Entreß is afraid that he might catch a cold. He is standing near the window, wearing a long coat which is buttoned up below his neck. He is wearing a cap on his head. He is a gaunt, tall man with a long face, wearing horn-rimmed glasses. The color of his face seems to be oddly in harmony with the color of the death skull (*Totenkopf*) which is placed on his cap. Dr. Diem, the prisoner physician, is standing next to him, holding the records of the sick.

Our line positions in a circle and the examination begins. Entreß is looking more at the papers which Dr. Diem is handing to him than at the prisoners who are passing by him. From time to time, his eyes will rest on a sick man when he is giving the order "Stop!"

After that a second order comes: "Bend your knees!"

His pale eyes slowly scrutinize the curved person. "Move on!"

The record card remains in the hand of the "camp physician." At the end of the inspection of the sick, he has already quite a few in his hand. . . .

After a "march past," we returned to hall number 7. A few minutes of waiting follow. Finally . . . The *Lagerälteste* of the hospital barracks, Hans Bock, prisoner number 5, entered. Although he wore a green corner, he was well liked among the prisoners. He was holding three notes in his hand, which had numbers written on them.

"Attention! Those who will be called may get their clothing and move on to the Block."

A few numbers followed. Those who were called left the hall. Bock took the second note.

"Those whom I am going to call now will be admitted to the hospital barracks."

Among others, I also heard my number. I am overcome by a joyful feeling. I am sure that a few days of rest will be awaiting me. I am already imagining myself lying in a warm bed where one may rest from early in the morning to late at night. A miracle!

Bock is now taking the third note into his hand:

"Those who are called now, line up in a double row!" he is saying with a changed voice. I look at George. He is lowering his head and is acting as if he were looking at his boots. "Something seems to be wrong," I quickly thought.

Only later did I learn the truth. Those prisoners who were listed on the last note would be given "shots." Those were the ones whose records had remained in the hands of Entreß during the inspection.

A shot meant d e a t h!

Those whom the camp physician had marked as unfit for work were sentenced to death. They were placed in double lines and led to Block number 20. There, in the washroom, they were already expected by the *Sanitätsunteroffizier* of the camp, *SS-Oberscharführer* Klehr, who was accompanied by an assistant.

The entering prisoner was seated on a stool. Klehr's assistant, Panszczyk, clasped the hands on the prisoner's back so that he could not make the slightest move. "Professor" Klehr, as he was called in the camp, was holding a syringe which had been prepared in advance. It was filled with phenol. All of a sudden, with a skillful motion, he stabbed the needle into the prisoner's heart and pressed down the piston.

A few convulsions and the pallbearers throw the corpse into a corner of the room, where they placed a cover over him. A moment later, the next patient entered.

The record about which "Professor" Klehr boasted in front of his colleagues consisted of sixty persons who, within an hour, had been finished off by injection.

10

The few restful days which I had anticipated when I entered the hospital barracks had now turned into an extended "vacation." The prisoners who were responsible for Block 20, where I was lying, medical attendants and physicians for prisoners, continually diagnosed new illnesses in me which were used as a pretext to keep me on the Block longer. They also offered similar help to other comrades from the SK. Later it actually became customary that a man from the SK, regardless of the condition of his health, was dismissed from the hospital barracks only after the date of his discharge from the SK had been determined. Thus, for the winter, my stay was secured, and for the spring, I counted on my discharge from the SK.

With the change of my personal situation, my fields of interest also changed. The ghosts of the club and the chimney of the crematory, which were so closely associated with the life of an SK man, were replaced by other, more pleasant thoughts. Now it was "important" which comrade would appear during the course of the day, and what he would bring, and who in the "diarrhea hall" would win the championship in the chess contest, or when the hall commandant would invite the "artists" to perform, etc. (The "artists" were convicted professional actors who would entertain their sick comrades in their spare time.)

These "days of paradise" passed away quickly and turned into weeks and months. Before I realized it, the winter passed by, and I was slowly preparing to return to the SK. There I intended, as soon as I had the chance, to report to the *Lagerführer* and place before him my request for a discharge from the SK.

One day in February, I woke up with a terrible headache and a high fever. I was unable to keep down my breakfast, or my lunch, which my comrades had imposed on me. I vomited as soon as I had eaten it. It was decided to send me down to the ground floor for an examination.

Toward midday, two friends and a medical orderly led me to number 5, where a physician, who was also a prisoner, was on duty. On the way, I suddenly became very dizzy, and I sank unconsciously into the arms of my comrades.

The next day, I woke up in the typhoid-fever hall. The typhoid fever which was raging in the camp at this time did not spare me. On the fifth day, to make matters worse, another misfortune came along: I had also developed meningitis.

Again, I lost my consciousness; this time for about three weeks. On a morning in March, I woke up, emaciated, starved, and punctured by injections. During the following days, I listened to what were now the "historical" reports about my illness. These indicated that I had already been with both feet in the "other" world. My strong body and the warm care of my comrades, as well as that of the physicians and medical attendants, had saved me.

After the fever subsided, I weighed about forty kilograms. I had lost half of my weight.

My plans to return to the SK occupied me anew. After another two weeks, I had at least enough strength to be able to go to the toilet without any help from a medical attendant.

One day, Dr. Szymanski, who had cared for me, rushed into my room, obviously upset.

"Quick! Get out of bed!"

In no way was I ready for a rush. Phlegmatically, I looked at him.

"What is the matter?"

"I'll explain this to you later; come on now!"

I crawled out of my bed as well as I could, and, wrapped in a blanket, I followed the physician. We landed in the toilet.

"Remain seated here until I fetch you back into the hall," he said to me before he disappeared.

A while later, I heard it called out in the corridor: "Attention!" Then there was a noise from some people rushing back and forth. Thereafter, it became quiet again.

I was sitting! A quarter of an hour passed, a half hour, a whole hour, an hour and a half, and I was still sitting in the same spot, where Dr. Szymanski had placed me.

After a good two hours, I again heard it called out: "Attention!" and soon thereafter, I saw my protector standing in the door. His face was beaming with contentment.

"It worked!" he called out loudly, standing right on the threshold: "You are alive!"

I looked at him stupidly.

"I know I am still alive! But if you would have let me sit here for two more hours, then in all likelihood, they would have had to carry me out."

"Come on. Let's go to the hall. I'll tell you everything!"

During the next quarter of an hour, I was informed about the true reason for the nervousness and later joy of Dr. Szymanski. Quite unexpectedly, the news had been announced from the *Schreibstube* of the hospital that *SS-Obersturmführer* Entreß wanted to conduct an inspection of our Block. Since the prisoners quite obviously distrusted the different SS men who would visit the patients, Dr. Szymanski thought it prudent to hide a few of his patients, including myself, during the time of the visit. It later turned out that this mistrust was very well founded.

Entreß had all patients who were introduced to him divided into three groups; during the following days, the first group was "liquidated" with an injection by "Professor" Klehr; the patients with typhoid fever belonged to this group. On March 19 the second group was transferred to the newly built camp of Birkenau, where ninety percent of them were "finished off." The third group remained in the hospital barracks.

This was the beginning of the later notorious "depopulation action" *(Entvölkerungsaktion)* in the hospital and the elimination of the typhoid epidemics.

The "success" of the visits to all hospital blocks can be expressed in the following numbers: About twenty-five prisoners were "wasted by injection." A thousand prisoners were sent to Birkenau. After three weeks, only eighty people were still alive there.

From this day onwards, similar visits were conducted at regular intervals. The consequence of this was that those with typhoid fever or with other contagious illnesses no longer reported for registry in the hospital. They endured their illnesses until they collapsed, totally debilitated and never to get up again. That happened at work as well as on the Block.

The situation in the hospital barracks now became so uncertain that I decided, despite my weakness, to return to the SK.

In the meantime, however, the entire SK of Auschwitz was transferred to Birkenau, which was several kilometers away.

A few days prior to the next "inspection of the sick," I remained in the recovery hall, where my friends took devoted care of me. Then one day, I put on my camp clothing with the proscribing black spot below the number which I had not worn for a long time. I reported to the orderly room of the camp (*Lagerschreibstube*). After a while, I was added to the group of prisoners which was assigned to Birkenau, and I marched on.

The new camp was quite pathetic in comparison with the extended Camp of Auschwitz. A number of barracks, which had been built hastily on a marshy terrain, were lacking the most primitive arrangements. There was no path, no water, no toilets. In other words: Everything that had been built in Auschwitz during the last years, at the expense of the blood of the thousands of victims, was lacking. There were no floors on the blocks, and quite often one would sink up to one's ankles into soft clay soil.

Aside from the SK and the rest of the transported patients, there were, in Birkenau, the survivors of the great transport of Russian prisoners of war. At the end of September, 12,000 men had been delivered. In March, only a total of 450 persons were counted among those who had survived. The camp bureaucrats obviously seemed to have given up hope for a normal "liquidation" of this rest. Therefore, they were transferred to Birkenau, which at that time enjoyed the sad reputation that it would "liquidate" all of its inmates. The camp bureaucrats were therefore not disappointed when the "remaining stock" of the Russians had been diminished to 100 men after two months, and after about a year, only forty strong men remained in the camp. Their Russian shirts reminded us that some time ago Russian prisoners of war had been delivered here.

The Punishment Company (SK) was placed in Block 3 at the beginning. After a few days, however, we were assigned to Block 1. This was a constructed barrack, the walls of which consisted of thin, single-layered bricks. One entered the inside through a door in the middle of the barrack. A rather wide corridor branched off to the right and left. On both sides of the corridor, there were three-storied sleeping bunks. Each bunk was two meters wide and one meter and eighty centimeters long. According to ordinance, six prisoners had to sleep in one such "bunk" and, in times of an overflow, ten or twelve people. Between the roof and the walls there were ten centimeter-wide gaps through which air, rain, and, later, snow had free access. In the entire barrack there was not a single window, there was no oven, and the toilets were in the square which was enclosed with a wall three meters high. "Toilet" is here a very flattering description of the ordinary iron carts which were placed under the wall. Sometimes five "interested people" were sitting there simultaneously.

Like our camp, our "protectors" also changed. Instead of Gerlach, *SS-Rottenführer* Sternberg now became *Blockführer* and *Kommandoführer*. He was a small, stocky type with abnormally long hands and a strange, small head sitting on a short, thick neck. During his short stay, which lasted only three weeks, he singlehandedly strangled about a hundred prisoners. Most of the time, they were the so-called "bodily weak" ones. After three weeks, *SS-Oberscharführer* Moll replaced him. He later became chief of the crematory and the gas chamber. He was a giant churl with tremendous physical strength, blond hair, and fresh blue eyes.

Instead of Hansens, an old criminal from Bavaria, named Rudolf, became the *Blockälteste*; he wore the number 15654. The infamous *Stubenälteste* Wacek was replaced by the former police informer Kmitas from Upper Selesia; the "red gangster" Gustav, prisoner number 3267, became *Oberkapo* of the SK; his helpers were Willi Brackmann, Arno Neumann, Karl "Dachdecker" (number 3216), and a few less known "green ones," as we called those with the green corners.

During this time, *SS-Hauptscharführer* Fitze became *Lagerführer* of Birkenau, and *SS-Unterscharführer* Schillinger became *Rapportführer*.

During the first night, I slept wonderfully in the new dwelling. The next day, I stood again in the eighth work-column, once more ready for new work. . . .

11

The new assignment of the SK consisted of digging up a channel, the so-called "king's ditch," which was to connect the Weichsel—the Vistula River—with its former riverbed. The channel was a few kilometers long and was situated between two sand banks, the purpose of which was to prevent flooding. We worked on a section of about four hundred meters, with each group consisting of twenty prisoners. Some were digging up the channel bed with shovels, others were binding together brushwood, and still others were completing the trenched channel by securing the banks with brushwood.

The entire section was secured by a number of SS guards, with the exception of those groups that were led by the *Kapos* Karl "Dachdecker" and Adolf Baginsky. In the camp, both had the reputation of being murderers. During the assignment of groups, when a man in a somewhat weak condition was assigned to their group, one could be certain that two hours later he would be carried in front of the "hut."

A favorite method of Karl was to strangle the people in water. He would single out a certain prisoner and order him to bend down. Since the *Kapos* had the authority to punish immediately by beating, such a prisoner thought that this was meant for the usual "twenty-five." Therefore, he stretched out his buttocks. This entire "ceremony" was usually carried out near the trenches, which were filled with water. In a given moment, Karl's club began to hit him, not on his buttocks but on his neck. Usually, the person who was struck that way fell unconsciously to the ground. Thereupon, *Kapo* Baginsky would appear and together they carried the unconscious person to the trench. There they ducked his head under water until death occurred.

Such "operations" were repeated several times a day. The victims of those henchmen were mostly new arrivals who were not yet familiar with our conditions. The long-established prisoners of the SK attempted to get into other, safer groups. These groups too were led by *Kapos* with green corners, but they behaved more calmly. *Kapo* Willi Brachmann was one of such 'calm" persons.

It so happened that I, too, worked with him. My friend in the camp, Kukla (number 702), worked in the warehouse for foodstuffs. Since *Kapo* Willi loved to eat SS sausages, I was given a magnificent job. On this job, I was sitting on a wooden block, and I had to use an ax to sharpen wooden pegs with which the brushwood was later secured. "With this work, I could survive the SK," I thought. I let the sun shine on my limbs, which had become pale during my stay in the hospital barracks.

At the end of May, a large group of "new arrivals," consisting of about 380 prisoners, arrived from the camp.

Most of them were "old numbers." They had arrived in the Punishment Company (SK) for the following reasons: One day, the names of about five hundred prisoners were called out. Some of them, 120 men, were led to Block 11 and were executed. The other 380 prisoners were being transferred to us. Their clothing was marked with additional "red dots." That meant that their bearers were, according to the Gestapo, especially politically dangerous, and were therefore in need of "special treatment," i.e., *Sonderbehandlung*. . . .

A few days passed quietly. The *Kommandoführer* Moll was obviously content with the new "arrivals." Work was proceeding fast, and a commission that came to inspect the work place one day praised the efficient completion of the work plan.

The newcomers were at first quite uneasy about the tragic end of their 120 comrades. As time passed, however, they became more relaxed. The Company, living in eternal fear, was even relieved because the new arrivals brought a new spirit and new life into the company.

After about a week, eight men who wore red dots were summoned during the morning roll call. They were transferred to Auschwitz. The next day we learned that they had been executed on Block 11.

Two days later, during the morning roll call, ten more "red-dot bearers" were summoned and sent to Auschwitz. Again, the news arrived that they had been executed.

When such a selection of men had already been sent to Auschwitz three times, we all realized that the bearers of the red dots were convicted to death. The leaders of the camp were merely afraid to carry out a mass execution of five hundred men; therefore, they wanted to achieve the same goal during shorter time intervals.

The mood in the camp became increasingly depressed. The "red-dot bearers" were clearly distinct from all others. During every free moment, one could see groups of these prisoners whispering while they were walking up and down. They interrupted their conversations the moment they saw a stranger approaching. During work, they were doubly industrious. Their groups, which consisted of only these men, worked breathlessly, strangely willing, without being driven on by the *Vorarbeiter*.

The result was that after a few days we already changed our workplace and came close to the location where the channel made quite a sharp turn. Work usually lasted until 5:00 p.m. Around this time, the whistle of the *Kommandoführer* announced the end of work. After this signal, all groups carried their working tools to the huts and lined up for the march-off.

June 10, 1942, was an exceptionally beautiful day. The sun was shining brightly, and there was not a single little cloud in the blue sky. The prisoners were moving more lively in the warm rays of the sun. Some took off their jackets, and, with their sleeves rolled up, they threw shovelfuls of dry, warm earth out of the trench.

After lunch, the entire Company reclined in the grass in order to rest a few more minutes in the warm sun before the end of the break

Like all the others, I looked for a spot where I could lie down. I placed my jacket under my head and tried to enjoy the short yet precious lunch break. I had hardly lain down when one of the "red-dot bearers," prisoner Lachowicz, came to me.

"Are you sleeping?"

"No, I am dancing!" I grumbled impatiently.

"Move over a bit." Lachowicz tossed his jacket to the ground, and a while later he was lying beside me. He looked silently at me for a while, and then he looked around. The next prisoner was lying at a distance of about fifteen meters.

"Nice weather," he said congenially. Impatiently, I raised my head.

"I acknowledge your detailed observations. However, go to hell," I answered grumpily. However, Lachowicz moved closer to me.

"Shut up!" He looked meaningfully into my eyes and added quietly: "We are bolting out today!"

I felt my blood rushing to my head. "What do you mean by 'we'?" I uttered briefly.

"I think that all . . .?" He closed his eyes and continued whispering, "It does not make any sense at all to wait until they lead us out, one by one, to number 11. What do you think about this?" Again he gazed at me with a sharp look. His clear, dark eyes were flashing strangely.

I was so confused about this news that I was unable to think clearly. It was simply unbelievable.

Lachowicz looked uninterruptedly at me. His eyes were filled with expectation and defiance.

"Well, are you coming with us?" he asked in a decisive tone.

Suddenly, I was overwhelmed. The next moment, I understood everything. Escape! That was the secret dream of every prisoner. I felt my heart pounding and my face turning hot. I nodded. "I come with you!"

Lachowicz's eyes beamed. "I knew it!" Forcefully he slapped my shoulders. "Listen! Yesterday, I received news from Auschwitz that all "red-dot bearers" had been sentenced to death. Be that as it may, no one will be able to rescue himself. We have nothing to lose. Outside the camp, everything is already prepared. On the other side of the Vistula, trucks will be waiting. And here everything is also ready. I am working with my group near the forest. Before the *Kommandoführer* will be blowing the whistle, all groups will have to pass by me in order to get into the room for the tools. I have decided with my comrades that at the moment when the whistle is blowing, they will have to be at the location where I am working since that will be the point of departure of our escape. Together with my boys, I am going to disarm the guard, and then we run quickly up to the wall. That will be a signal for the rest. Everyone will have to reach the Vistula on his own." He interrupted himself for a short while and lowered his head. "Of course, we are counting on casualties as well. I estimate that about two hundred men will be shot or captured during the escape. Despite that, an additional two hundred will remain alive. And if only fifty men will remain alive—it will still be worthwhile. These fifty men will gain life, which is lost for them in this place."

A new thought occurred to me.

"That is all very well. What, however, is the regular SK to do? How should those who do not wear a red dot react?"

"They will have to come with us. You are about forty or fifty men. If you are still going to remain here after the escape, they will certainly get rid of you as 'retaliatory measures.' . . . I have thought about that for a long time," he added apologetically. "There is no other alternative. Only ten percent of all men in the SK have a chance of holding out. We will be executed with bullets—you will be finished off with clubs. There is no other alternative."

That was a correct and convincing consideration. We still exchanged a few words, during which time I was informed about the details of the escape, when a whistle announced the end of the lunch break. The groups returned to their work, and I again took my place at the sharpening of the wooden pegs.

Only now was I able to form clear thoughts, to consider every *pro* and *con,* and recover from my excitement, which was still controlling my feelings. The plan was undoubtedly a good one, and it would— as Lachowicz had planned—in all probability be successful.

It was really hopeless to just sit here. Reflecting on it rationally, it seemed nonsensical to always be counting on the turn of fortune. This feeling had never left me during my stay in the camp. Every day, every hour, every minute, this luck could be reversed. A mood, any idea or simply the bad temper of a *Kapo* or SS man would be sufficient to erase my number from the card register of the living prisoners, as had already been done to ten thousands of detainees. . . .

Here, with this plan, everything would be quickly and finally decided. If the escape were successful, I would certainly regain my life. If it should fail, then I would at least lose with the knowledge that I would not have saved my life anyway by remaining in the camp. . . .

My thoughts were calm, collected and cold-blooded. With my right hand I sharpened the wooden pegs as never before.

Three hours still remained until the whistle of the *Kommandoführer*, which would also signal the escape. A-hundred-and-eighty minutes! I was amused by this kind of counting because I remembered the first months in the camp. At that time, I did not count according to months but rather according to days. Fifty days or a hundred and fifty; that already sounded much more serious and gave rise for new hope If I have survived so long already, and I am still alive—then I would think that everything else will henceforth go well also. . . .

And indeed, it was not bad at all. One could even say it was "wonderful" because I am still alive. . . .

However, what will be in one-hundred-and-eighty minutes?

There are already fewer minutes now—and still fewer. My axe works vigorously at the wood.

Just now, *Kommandoführer* Moll is coming out of the hut. He is stepping onto the hill with the expression of a ruler on his face. He is observing the work area. After a while, he notices that something might not be quite right with one group, and he rapidly moves towards it. Shortly thereafter, I hear curses. . . .

"It will be interesting to see what kind of face *Herr* Moll will be making in less than three hours" crosses my mind.

With satisfaction, I continue the sharpening.

However, how shall it take place now?

At the moment of the whistle, which will announce the end of work, Lachowicz should run to the wall and toss his jacket into the air. . . .

The group of prisoners should be nearby under the leadership of those who are informed, and, according to this signal, everyone should rush into the wall. . . . At the other side, the entire area, almost up to the Vistula, is covered with a thick, young forest which is interspersed with shrubs. The Vistula is quite shallow at this point, and at the other side of the bank, freedom is waving. . . .

Freedom!

I took a deep breath. The air smelled different than at other times. It was filled with the fragrance of freedom!

A moment ago, *Kapo* Willi Brachmann came with three prisoners in order to fetch the finished pegs. I decided to take advantage of this opportunity.

"Willi, what time is it already?"

He looked at his watch. "Ten minus before three o'clock."

That means fifty minutes have already passed. So quickly! Around four o'clock Lachowicz passed by me.

"Is everything okay?" he asked briefly, while walking by.

I nodded with my head.

He moved on to the other groups.

Thus the seconds passed, they turned into minutes and, unavoidably, they brought the fifth hour. The faster the time elapsed, the more nervous I became. I could no longer think straight. I was irritated and felt a tickle in my fingertips. I am sure I had red cheeks and feverish eyes. Although I could not look at myself, I sensed it.

Still fifty minutes . . . For the third time already, I went to the hut in order to cast a glance at the clock which was hanging there.

Forty minutes . . . They pass unusually slowly now. Each minute seems to be longer now than five minutes two hours ago. I clean up my workplace. I organize the sharpened wooden pegs into small heaps of thirty pieces.

When it will be a quarter to five o'clock, I shall walk with such a bundle toward Lachowicz's group. They are now working right near the wall and are bundling scrub wood.

Still, thirty-five minutes . . . All of a sudden, the sky is quite unexpectedly beginning to change. Heavy, dark clouds are building up. No one knows where they are coming from. A strong wind is rising.

I am happy about that. In rainy weather, Moll and his SS men will not be all that careful.

It is starting to rain. First drop by drop, then the drops become bigger, and finally it is pouring, as if from buckets.

The Company continues to work. According to our supervisors, rain does not constitute an obstacle to work. I button up my jacket up to my neck, and at that moment I notice that the door to the hut is opening and Moll is appearing in its frame. Moll looks for a while at all the shapes of the prisoners, who duck in the rain. I do not take my eyes off him. He is turning slowly, is looking at his watch, and is reaching into his pocket. I am turning pale. I clearly feel how every drop of blood moves out of my face. Moll is holding the whistle in his hand, is lifting it to his mouth, and a long, shrill whistle-blow is rending the air asunder.

End of work!

And the clock turns half past four o'clock. . . .

I move my head toward the direction where Lachowicz is working with his group. They are by themselves, and the distance to the next group is about three hundred meters.

Now what?

What will Lachowicz do now? The previously prepared plan, I am sure, will be carried out. I feel cold drops of sweat on my forehead and stand motionlessly, as if hypnotized!

And suddenly . . . From the direction of the wall, I hear a scream and see a jacket being tossed into the air. A few prisoners storm onto the wall. The figure of the guard disappears, and shortly thereafter, I see that he is lying on the ground. The escapees run over him and past him. I quickly look around. The distance between me and the location for the escape is about two hundred meters. A few meters away from me, Moll is standing there, entirely confused. If I move away from the spot, I thought in a split second, he will blast a bullet into my head.

From all sides, the prisoners come running in total confusion. The SS guards throw away their guns and run along the wall. I clearly see shades that are walking over the wall and disappear on the other side. Suddenly, Karl "Dachdecker," along with other *Kapos*, appear high up on the wall. He is holding an axe in his hand and is yelling inhumanly. A few meters away from him, the prisoner Pajaczkowski climbs onto the wall. Karl throws himself on him. For a while, they are wrestling with each other. Then Pajaczkowski is hit by Karl's club and is falling to the ground.

This moment was decisive. The other prisoners, who are running in the direction of the wall, stopped all of a sudden, and *Kommandoführer* Moll remembers now that he has a pistol. He began to shoot, whereupon the other guards on their posts opened fire with machine guns.

The bullets were whistling around the ears of the escapees. One prisoner, who had been struck, began to scream desperately, but Karl's hysterical bellowing drowned out the noise.

The order came. "Lie down!" Thereupon, one could hear the shrill voice of *Kommandoführer* Moll:

"For every head that is lifted up, there will be a bullet! Everyone will have to lie down, flat on their face, with the snout on the ground!"

The shooting still lasted for another quarter of an hour, despite the fact that they already had the situation under control. The loudest noise came from the SS men who had been the first to throw away their guns as they had begun to flee. Then silence set in because they were finally out of ammunition. Shorty thereafter Moll gave a new order:

"*Kapos* and *Vorarbeiter,* and those wearing green corners, line up!"

About forty men came together.

"You are going to help me with the roll call and with the counting. You have the right to kill anyone who looks suspicious and seems to have dangerous intentions. Hurry up now!"

Moll's helpers set to work with barbaric bellowing. We were placed in rows of hundreds, and after we had been counted, there came again the order, "Lie down!" Each row of one hundred prisoners was immediately surrounded by a section of SS men and by those who wore green corners.

Each attempt to lift one's head ended in death. Within the next ten to fifteen minutes about fifteen prisoners lost their lives because of curious glances or because of too obvious movements.

At one point, when Moll, with an unlocked pistol, walked by a group of prisoners who were lying down, one of them, suffering from diarrhea, attempted to rise up, asking permission to go to the toilet. Moll did not hesitate long. He placed the pistol at the prisoner's head and pulled the trigger. Blood and part of the brain splashed from the skull, riddled with bullets, onto those who were lying next to him. After half an hour, the counting was finished, and it was noted that twenty prisoners were missing. In addition to those, there were two prisoners who had been captured while they were jumping over the wall. Both had been beaten until they were unconscious. They were not killed because they were to be used for the interrogation.

Kommandoführer Moll gave a short but "vigorous" speech. He said that we were all dumb dogs, that we were wrong to think that this escape could have been successful, and finally that all of us were responsible. Afterwards, we were surrounded by a double chain of guards, and we marched away in the direction of the camp. On the way, we met a few cars with SS men, who were armed to their teeth. They drove to the location of the turmoil in order to search for the escapees. In a special car, there was a pack of police dogs.

In a very bleak mood, we returned to the camp. In the square of the Block, we took position as if to stand at attention. Moll gave the *Kapos* the order to search our bodies. The smallest pocket knife was considered a weapon. After a few minutes of having been "worked over," one owner of a knife was carried below the wall.

After this "visitation," our numbers were called out. Those who were called were positioned into lines of ten, as if to stand at attention. In this manner, the names of the escapees were determined.

Towards evening Moll returned once more. He ordered that the daily rations, which in the meantime had arrived, be sent back to the kitchen. Again he gave a speech:

"I know that the escape was prepared for a long time. If you do not reveal the names of the organizers by tomorrow morning, the entire Punishment Company (SK) will be executed. Understood?"

"Yes, Sir!"

"Dismissed to the Blocks."

After a few minutes, we were lying silently in our bunks, filled with horror. . . .

12

THE NEXT MORNING, BEFORE the roll call, we were divided into two groups. One of them consisted of all those with red dots; the other included the rest of the prisoners.

During the roll call, the "red-dot bearers" formed the right wing; we took the place near the gate. After the *Blockälteste* had inspected the *Rapportbuch*, the order came:

"The old SK get ready for the march to work! The red dots remain behind!"

The relatively small number of the original SK lined up quickly in rows of five in the direction of the exit gate. We were eighty men altogether; a third of those were overseers, *Kapos* and *Vorarbeiter*. Their facial expressions were foreboding. I looked around. At the end of the column stood my protector, Willi Brachmann. Seized by a premonition, I went to him.

"Willi . . !"

"What is the matter?"

"I am so weak today. Do you think I might be able to remain on the Block under a pretext?"

Willi looked at me with surprise.

"Are you crazy? In this hell? Do you have any idea what will be happening here today?"

"I do not have a red dot! I shall remain on the Block as a sick man. And after all . . . Perhaps I might be able to go into the kitchen to fetch water. Apparently a new transport with SS sausages has arrived in the storeroom!"

This argument convinced my conversation partner. He led me to the *Blockältesten,* and the matter regarding my stay was decided in my favor.

In addition to me, there were other bearers of the "black dot" on the Block. They were construction workers, who prepared the rooms for the

Blockältesten, two night watchmen, and the *Stubenälteste*. We were standing at the door, engaged in a lively conversation. All at once, quite unexpectedly, *Blockführer* Moll appeared. He entered so suddenly that we had no time to disperse. He looked at us with hostility, and then he yelled:

"*Blockältester*!" The startled Rudolf reported: "As ordered, present on the spot!"

"What are these dogs doing here?" He pointed at us. "Everyone outside into the square!"

Instead of giving us a chance to explain our presence on the Block, the *Blockälteste* jumped into our group, gave the one nearest him a blow to his teeth and bellowed loudly:

"Everyone into the square! But fast!"

A minute later, we formed the first line of ten of the "red-dot bearers"!

After the inspection of the Block, Moll appeared in the door again. "What? You cursed bandits are still standing? Everyone bend their knees!" The order was carried out in a flash.

"Well, did you think about it overnight? Who has something to tell me?" He continued to scream while his small pig eyes scrutinized the lines. An overall silence was the answer.

"Well, we shall see!" he continued sneeringly. "Soon the *Lagerführer* will be here. Then we shall speak another language."

He turned around and walked to the gate.

After a while, I got up and went to the *Blockältesten*.

"What do you want here?"

"I would like to clarify a misunderstanding," I began, but a well-aimed punch in the chin shoved the rest of the sentence back into my throat.

"Get lost! I am not in the mood to get into trouble because of you. Get in line!"

During my absence my place had been taken, and I was forced to be the first in line. After a few minutes, the door guard, who had watched the camp street through a hole in the door, yelled:

"The *Lagerführer* is coming!"

Rudolf nervously straightened out his jacket, removed the cap from his head, and yelled at us:

"Attention: Get still lower on your knees!"

In the next minute, the green uniforms of those who entered were glistening in the open gate. They were all VIPs from Auschwitz. Ahead of them all marched the successor of Fritzsch, the *Lagerführer* of all camps belonging to Auschwitz, *SS-Hauptsturmführer* Aumeier, an inconspicuous little figure wearing shiny boots, with a huge pistol dangling down from his belt to his knees. He was followed by the *Arbeitsdienstführer, SS-Hauptsturmführer* Schwarz, behind him followed *SS-Unterscharfüher* Heßler, *SS-Hauptscharführer* Palitzsch, Fitze, the chief of the "political section," *Kriminalobersekretär, SS-Unterscharführer* Grabner, and at the end our *Block-* and *Kommandoführer* Moll. A short report of the *Blockältesten* follows. Then Aumeier inspects, with long energetic steps, the front of the Block, whereby his small figure gives a somewhat comical impression. He stops a few meters from where I am standing. The pack of his body guards obediently halts behind him. I really experience a choking in my throat, a suffocating feeling when I breathe. Theatrically, Aumeier places his hands on his hips.

"You cursed bandits!" he is snapping at us. He has a piping, screeching voice. "You attempted an uprising, did you?" He is breathing faster. One can notice how he becomes heated over his own words. "I shall show you an uprising, you cursed dogs!" He is interrupting his words for a moment, and, with his small moving eyes, he is looking down at the lines of those in squatting positions, and suddenly, with a jump, he comes near me. At that moment, I feel the blood rushing into my face. It is turning black before my eyes. All that is lasting for a fraction of a second. Quickly, I am controlling myself and lift my head a bit higher. Aumeier seizes the prisoner who is sitting next to me in a squatting position by his collar. He is pulling him up.

"Well, you rabid dog! Tell me, who has organized the uprising?" In the meantime, his bony, small hand unbuttons the case of his pistol. The young, twenty-year-old boy, whom he had seized out of the line, is as white as a sheet. He has big, azure eyes with which he looks motionlessly to the ground. His bloodless lips are pressed tightly together.

"You don't wont to answer, you dog?" His bony finger rips a long revolver out of the case, "Do you see this?" The long barrel is hitting the boy on his nose. "Who was it who organized the escape from the king's ditch?"

The prisoner's lips are pressed together even more tightly. They almost disappear. Aumeier's question remains unanswered. About four hundred prisoners observe this, holding their breath. The *Lagerführer* still does not give up. He is placing the revolver on the extended chest of the prisoner.

"I am giving you a last chance to save your life. I am going to count to three. If you do not answer my question, I am going to shoot you like a dog. Do you understand?"

Silence . . .

"Who has organized the escape?" Aumeier's voice screeches, hisses, and gnashes, sounding as if one were sharpening a knife on a glass.

Silence . . .

"I am going to start counting. One . . ."

The boy's chest begins to move somewhat faster. His eyes are frozen in terrible fright.

"Two . . ."

Someone from the middle of the first row is fainting. He is falling down in front of the line. His eyes are half closed, and foam is running down to the ground from his half-open mouth.

"Three . . ." The bony finger of the *Lagerführer* is drawing the trigger of the revolver. . . .

A shot is falling.

The boy convulses unnaturally; he inhales powerfully with his wide-open mouth. He takes half a turn, and suddenly he is falling to the ground like a block of wood. Smoke is still coming from the barrel of the pistol. Aumeier yells at Moll:

"Read out the first ten names on the list loudly. But fast!"

Moll reaches nervously into his pocket, draws out some sort of papers, flicks through them, and finally calls out:

"13486!"

"Here!" The voice of the one who is called is responding from the last row.

"Come forward!"

In this same way, the ten men come forward. Their faces look towards the Block; their backs are turned toward those in a squatting position. The SS men stand between them and us. Aumeier moves forward. He is standing one meter away from those who were called up. Again he places his hands on his hips.

"Did you see?" His hand is pointing to the dead boy lying on the ground. "You all will end up like this if you are trying to resist us. I shall give you one minute so that you can make your statements. . . ." He places his revolver back into the case and looks at his watch. Only fifty seconds . . . Then he walks around the standing group and moves towards the SS men. Whispering, he speaks with Palitzsch and Heßler, and then he calls Moll and gives him inaudible orders.

All three draw their pistols.

Aumeier returns to the ten men who are silent.

"Well, did you think about it?!"

Silence . . . Now Aumeier signals with his hand. Palitzsch, Heßler, and Moll position themselves with their shining weapons behind the first three of the standing prisoners.

"Well, you don't want to talk," the *Lagerführer* acknowledges while he moves cautiously to the right side. "Well. . ." He waves with his hand for the second time.

Just then, three shots are fired. Three bodies fall to the ground with a thud. Those who did the shooting move behind the next three.

"Well, have you not yet decided?" Aumeier's voice sounds ironic. "I have time, and we have enough bullets." He signals anew with his hand.

Again, three shots, three horrible holes in the back of their heads, three dead men sink to the ground. . . .

The henchmen move on, as if they were marionettes.

"Well? You are still silent? You are only four men now. Are you ready to make a statement?"

Silence . . . Aumeier draws his pistol.

"Fire!" he is commanding his SS men, and he himself is shooting the fourth prisoner. He aims badly. The prisoner has been shot in his breast, and then he is standing motionlessly for a while until he suddenly begins to scream, terribly. *SS–Hauptscharführer* Palitzsch "professionally" makes up for the clumsiness of his superior. A shot from a distance of twenty centimeters silenced the prisoner. The eleventh body is falling to the ground. Around the head of each of those executed, a dark bloodstain is formed in the soil.

The henchmen return to the SS group, who calmly smoke their cigarettes and exchange their observations. They give the impression that they are theater guests who comment on the performance. Aumeier is also joining them.

The latest events do not seem to have affected him. With a self-assured motion, he is reaching for his cigarettes, is taking a match, is lighting a cigarette, and then he is observing for a while how it is burning out, and then he is blowing it out, is throwing it to the ground, and is taking a deep puff. Only then does he participate in the conversation.

The result is that ten other prisoners are called up. They are ordered to undress the ones who have been shot and to lay the corpses in one row near the entrance gate. After about twenty minutes, their work is done. Near the gate, there lie at one side a heap of bloodstained camp uniforms, and at the other side, there is a row of eleven human bodies, the oldest of whom might have been twenty-six years old.

When the prisoners tried to return to their rows, Aumeier retains them.

"Well, you might think that this is already all? Line up in one row!"

The story is repeated. After a few minutes, all of them are on the ground with bullets in their heads. The next ten prisoners return unhindered to their rows, after they have undressed the dead.

Obviously, Aumeier had enough. He calls the *Blockältesten*. Rudolf is reporting somewhat uncertainly and with chattering teeth.

"These dogs," the *Lagerführer* begins, "will not get anything to eat. If they have not decided to report their ringleaders by four o'clock, they will all be shot." He is speaking the last words loudly, and, while turning to us, he is asking:

"Did you understand?"

This time no one is answering him.

For a while, Aumeier looks at the lines with astonishment. Finally, he spits out and is walking in the direction of the gate. His SS bodyguard is following him. And behind them, the door is closing.

Then Rudolf began to wipe his perspiring forehead with a handkerchief.

"Good heavens . . . What a thing. . .!" He is shaking his head several times, and suddenly he assumes an unusually brave posture. "All of you sit down!" he bellowed. Yelling at the door guard, he said, "And you keep watch! If you should sight anyone, then give a sign!" Proud of his "brave" order, he went to the Block. It now began to be noisy in the square. Everyone was excited and talked in confusion. Some of the more serious prisoners gathered around the "latrine cart." They talked about something. Then one of them, Dr. Jablonowski from Warsaw came forward.

"Comrades, listen! There is no doubt that Aumeier will keep his word. After conferring with several comrades, we five men have decided to report to Moll with the intention of admitting that we were the organizers of the escape. . . ."

The lines of the prisoners fell silent.

Dr. Jablonowski continued, "In our opinion that will be the only possible way to rescue the rest, if, indeed, we can speak of a rescue. Those comrades who have decided with me to admit their guilt before Moll are fully aware of the fact that they will be executed. . . . I am saying this because in the case of success you ought not to develop a bad conscience because your life was saved at our expense. This will be all I wanted to say. . . ." He nodded and disappeared into the surging crowd.

Now everything was set into motion. From all sides, they pressed to Dr. Jablonowski to shake his hand and to thank him. Hope seized their hearts. The conversation became livelier, and one could not help feeling that the entire matter would now be resolved.

The *Blockälteste* to whom the prisoners' intention was reported shook his head again. "I don't understand this at all . . . to get voluntarily shot. . . That is really wonderful . . . but I could not have decided to do that." Despite that, he seemed to be inwardly moved by the intentions of these people. He disappeared into the Block and returned after a few moments with two loaves of bread and sausage.

"The five men who want to report to Moll, come here!" They pressed through the lines towards him.

"Here, every one of you will get half a loaf of bread and half a pound of sausage. But you have to eat it yourselves!" he added seriously.

Despite this request, bread and sausage was divided among those who were standing close by.

Toward noon, the *Arbeitskommando* returned from their work. On an old wagon, they brought nineteen corpses, corpses of those prisoners who had been finished off while working. It later became clear that immediately after leaving the Block, *Kommandoführer* Moll had driven with a motorcycle to the "king's ditch." Everything had gone very well until he arrived.

The *Kapos* and *Vorarbeiter* had been preoccupied with commenting on the events of the previous day and had not paid special attention to the working prisoners.

Immediately after his arrival, Moll summoned all special forces, and soon thereafter, they began their "work." During the course of the next quarter of an hour, almost half of the group was "finished off." I would not know to which group I would have belonged if I had gone to work. I still looked quite ill, and people with such an appearance had fallen as the first victims.

After lunch, the men of the old SK were driven to the Block and given orders to sleep. Of course, sleep was out of the question. Everyone was waiting in suspense for the fourth hour of the afternoon. A few minutes before four o'clock, a few *Kapos* were called into the courtyard. These were Karl "Dachdecker," Boginsky, Neumann and Brachmann. Through the gaps in the wall, we watched the actions in the square. The *Kapos* disappeared with Moll behind the gate. After some time, they returned, each carrying a large role of wire on his back, which they threw in front of the Block.

Toward four o'clock, *SS–Hauptscharführer* Fitze, the *Lagerführer* of Birkenau, and Schillinger, the *Rapportführer* of that Camp, appeared. Fitze carried a folder with papers under his arm. The small table of the *Blockältesten* and a chair were carried out of the Block. Fitze sat down and spread the papers out on the small table. Shortly thereafter, Schillinger ran to the gate, and when he returned, several SS men accompanied him. They carried machine-gun pistols, ready to fire. They took positions near the gate and lined up according to Schillinger's direction.

At this moment, Dr. Jablonowski, accompanied by his four comrades, approached the table. Fitze listened calmly, looked hard at all of them, and then said:

"It is to no avail. I no longer need your statements because all of you will be transported to Kattowitz. There you will be interrogated, one by one." He motioned his hand in refusal and concentrated again on his papers. Dr. Jablonowski and his comrades returned to their old places. Fitze got up.

"Listen! In order to conduct a just inquiry, you will all be taken to Kattowitz. There it will be determined who was responsible for yesterday's escape. You may rest assured that he who is found innocent will not lose a single hair from his head. In order to facilitate the transport, you will all be bound. Every prisoner whom I call should come to the table." He sat down again and motioned to the *Kapos*. In the meantime, they had rolled up the wire.

The calling of the names began. Everyone who was called went to the table, gave his particulars, and at the same time crossed his hands behind his back, which the *Kapos* skillfully bound together with the thin wire. With another piece of wire, five prisoners were bound to each other. After that, the men of the right and left flanks were bound together with the next row of five. Thus, they created a column wired together which consisted of about 340 people. When the last ones were "worked over", the entire column was surrounded by SS men, who were armed with submachine guns. Soon after that, the order rang out: "In step, forward march!"

Slowly and with rattling chains, the column moved in the direction of the gate. On the Block, a terrible silence set in. The monotonous marching steps pressed toward us through the gaps of the wall. In their horrible monotony, the marching steps sounded ghostly. When the last rows marched through the gate, we were quickly given our supper and sent to bed. Until late in the night, we discussed the "expedition" to Kattowitz. . . .

Early the next day, we learned during the coffee reception in the kitchen that all "red-dot bearers" were not taken by train to Kattowitz last night, but instead they were brought to a little house which was located two kilometers from the camp. There, during the night, they all were gassed. . . .

During the night, from the small forest which surrounded the house, bloody, grey fire tongues flared against the sky. . . .

13

A FEW DAYS LATER, while I was at work, I was summoned by *Kapo* Karl. He still had the reputation of liquidating the prisoners. Therefore, I did not obey his order. Instead, I went to Willi Brachmann. He listened calmly and said:

"You will have to disappear from the Company. Today I will keep you with me until the end of work."

While we were talking, "Dachdecker" ran angrily toward us. "Did you not hear that I gave you orders to report to me, didn't you?" He hit me on the head with his club and already took a second swing at me, when Willi seized his hand.

"For the time being, you leave him alone. I need him."

"That is not my problem. I have had it in for him for a long time."

Willi straightened up. "You should leave him alone for the time being!" he said quietly but with an explicit threat in his voice. During this time, Willi was considered for a promotion to *Oberkapo* in the SK. Therefore, Dachdecker gave up. He walked away cursing.

"Did you hear it?"

Without a word, I nodded.

"For today you are still safe, but for tomorrow I cannot guarantee anything. Inform your friends so that they can get you out of the Block."

I did not leave his side until the end of work. In the meantime, I wrote a short letter to Kukla:

> My dear!
> Willi thinks that I should vanish from the Company. If you are able to do something about my situation, I would like to ask you for your help. Karl "Dachdecker" tried to finish me off today, but Willi prevented it. Should you be able to do something, then we

> shall discuss this further. If not, then please do not forget, after you left the Camp, to greet my family. . . . Servus! 8214

On our return, when we walked by the kitchen, I gave this letter to a comrade, asking him to give it immediately to prisoner 702, named Kukla.

Until the evening I waited impatiently. I was unable to imagine how they would get me out of the Block. I was certain, however, that Kukla would set everything into motion in order to help me.

Every time the door opened, I jumped up, but until the sound of the gong, no one had come.

Resigned and with gloomy thoughts about what the next day would bring, I lay down to sleep. However, I couldn't sleep and tossed from one side to the other. I tried to tell myself that the next day would pass favorably, but that could not reassure me. As soon as I closed my eyes, I saw the figure of Karl with his fat belly and his evil eyes, in which one could no longer notice anything human. Images of Karl's actions moved in front of my eyes. The horrible scenes in which he choked other comrades emerged anew, and the terrifying certainty of the next day arose with horror in my imagination. . . .

Around eleven o'clock at night, the door suddenly creaked. Someone came to the Block. I held my breath and listened anxiously. They spoke quite loudly with the *Blockältesten,* and soon I heard that someone called out:

"The sick line up!"

Within the next minute, I was downstairs. Instinctively I felt that this was a rescue. In the corridor, next to the door, stood the chief medical attendant of the Camp, Jub Bernatzik, who was accompanied by the *Blockältesten.* Tottering, I moved close to them. As well as I could, I pretended to be sick, and began, with a trembling and breaking voice, to complain about headaches and nausea. No sooner had I finished my tale of woes when Karl suddenly appeared.

"What? This dog? He is as healthy as a bull. The laziest pig in the entire Company. It is out of the question that he . . ."

Jub Bernatzik looked at him from below his glasses.

"For the time being, no one is asking you for your opinion. I decide and not you, whether this prisoner is sick or healthy, and whether he is lazy or not does not concern me. And regarding your remark, 'It is out of the question,' it is out of the question that you interfere with my work!" He said all this with a calm and cool voice without taking his eyes from Karl. Then he reached into his pocket and pulled out a fever thermometer, looked at it, checked it, and shook it down, looked at it again, and, without a word, he put it into my armpit. When Jub continued to speak with the *Blockältesten* without even paying any attention to Karl, fear began to seize me. After all, I knew that I really had neither fever nor any other illness. I was afraid that Jub might want to pull out of the affair because he might not have any proof of any sickness. And in that case, I would have to stay on the Block with Karl. This possibility brought the next morning a few hours closer. Finally, Jub removed the fever thermometer. In the meantime, he had taken off his glasses, and therefore, he gave it to the *Blockältesten.*

"Look at it, Rudi, how many degrees?" . . .

At that moment, I really began to feel very hot. Rudi looked at it for a while and then said:

"Thirty-eight five!"

I was flabbergasted.

"Show me your tongue!" I heard Jub's voice.

Mechanically, I followed his order.

"Well, quite normal. Do you perhaps have pain in the area of your liver?"

Eagerly I nodded my head. "That is typical! Typhoid fever!" he determined. Then he turned to the *Blockältesten.* "Considering the danger of contagion for the Block, I am taking him to the hospital barracks immediately. Prepare a referral form for me quickly!"

While the *Blockälteste* disappeared into his room, Bernatzik turned to Karl:

"Well, what kind of fool are you now?"

Dachdecker spat angrily and walked away without a word. After a few minutes, I walked through the gate of Block "7." All prisoners who suffered from contagious diseases were transferred there. In addition, there were also prisoners from other Auschwitz camps who had been singled out for gassing because they were considered unfit for work.

In the orderly room of the *Blockältesten*, where Viktor Mordarski was, Kukla was already waiting for me. When he saw me, he winked, cleaned his glasses, patted me on the shoulders, and pulled out two "SS sausages" which he had hidden under his belt.

"It was successful! Okay! Here you have something to eat and don't lose your head. One can escape from any situation; one must only know how to master it appropriately." He turned to Bernatzik. "Did it go smoothly?" The chief medical attendant nodded seriously.

"The medical sciences have diagnosed typhoid fever, and the *Herr Blockälteste* informed us personally about the temperature." Then, speaking to me, he said, "Why are you looking at me so foolishly? You have typhoid fever! I really should put you to bed immediately. . . . I have a soft heart and a preference for blond people. I therefore permit you to stay with us longer."

"Only under the condition that the *Blockälteste* will, according to protocol, first delouse and disinfect our honorable admission," Kukla added jokingly. "Typhoid lice apparently prefer to go to people with fat bellies. . . ." He gave Bernatzik an important look. "Since my earliest childhood, I did not like typhoid fever!" He suddenly became very serious. "And you, *Blockältester*," he said, turning to Viktor, who had been silent until now, "Prepare for this corpse a respectable bunk with a straw sack and two blankets."

"Are you crazy? Whence shall I take a straw sack?"

Kukla turned up his nose.

"Well, your own, if there is no other solution. You like fish, I believe. Just this week, the *Kapo* of the fish commando has promised me a few kilograms, and during my last visit to the main stock room, I luckily 'noticed' a box with margarine. Well, what about it?"

Viktor crimsoned. "I really did not take him into our Block because I expected something in return from you," he started saying. But Kukla interrupted him. "I know. Perhaps out of sympathy for his green eyes. You cannot fool us, *Blockältester*. In a word: Does he get a straw sack and two blankets or not?" "He shall get them!"

"Now I like you! A pound of fish and a stick of margarine will be delivered tomorrow to your hermitage. And now, gentlemen, he who goes to bed late will yawn the entire day, and therefore, in this sense!" He patted me once more on the shoulders and disappeared. After a few minutes, I was assigned my sleeping place. I had an entire bunk to myself, a straw sack, and two rather heavy blankets. I wrapped them tightly around myself and was happy—perhaps for the first time in the camp! In my right hand, I had a piece of sausage which smelled wonderful, and in the left a quarter of a loaf of bread. I ate very slowly, and, with the certainty that no one would bother me, I relished every bite of it because such an SS sausage tasted by no means any different than those smoked sausages before the war. Long after midnight, I fell asleep.

14

Block number 7 was known in the camp as the "anteroom to the crematory." It was divided into four rooms. The first was occupied by those who were recovering and other "show-offs" like myself. The second room was designated for those with tuberculosis and prisoners with internal illness. The third room housed those with typhoid fever, and the fourth was for those who were ill with diarrhea and those who needed surgical intervention. In each of the rooms there were fifteen tripartite bunk beds which, according to common camp practice, were estimated to hold 270 patients. Theoretically, these four rooms were able to take in 1,080 patients. At the time of my arrival, the number of the sick consisted of over 1,800.

The medical staff consisted of the *Blockältesten*, Viktor Mordarski; the clerk, Eduard Piasecki; the medical attendants, Bogdan Glinski and Stephan; a young physician from Czechoslovakia; and finally the physician, Dr. Krause. The *Blockälteste* and the clerk were not assigned to the care of the sick because they were already overburdened with administrative work. Thus, there were only three medical attendants available for the care of the 1,800 patients. Unfortunately, after a few days, one of them, namely the Czech, also became sick with typhoid fever.

In the entire Block, there were about one hundred blankets and several straw sacks. There were no toilets or washrooms available. In fact, they were nowhere to be found in the entire Camp of Birkenau. The sick did not wash themselves, and their natural needs were carried out in the square which was enclosed by a high wall. Similarly, all prisoners of the entire SK relieved themselves of their natural urgent needs in this same way.

The monthly rations of medication which Dr. Krause had later at his disposal consisted of about fifteen paper bandages; one hundred grams of cotton, wool, gauze, and cellulose; as well as small containers of ointment, such as Ichtiol, and zinc ointment for scabies and other such ailments. In addition to that, there were a few grams of powder such as aspirin, tanalbin, coal, etc. Of course, these supplies had to last for an entire month. Under these conditions, the sick could not receive even minimal medical treatment. The entire work of Dr. Krause and Bogdans consisted merely of carrying the corpses out of the bunks and writing their numbers on their breasts. Indeed, the daily number of those who died amounted to eighty to one hundred people. However, since all the sick from all of the Camps of Auschwitz were committed to Block number 7, 150 to 200 "new arrivals" were admitted daily.

As I already mentioned in the previous chapter, all newly admitted sick prisoners were usually designated for gassing. The capacity for admissions to the provisional gas chambers in the small birch tree forest and to the crematory, where the gassed corpses were burned, consisted of 500 human bodies per week. The same number of the sick was always "removed" from our Block. After each "selection," over 1,000 candidates still remained, who, one by one, were anticipating their death. Their numbers increased weekly because of the new arrivals. And so it went on, week after week.

The things which I saw in Block number 7 surpassed everything I had ever seen until now in the camp. As soon as the sleeping bunks were filled, the new arrivals were laid down on the clay floor of the corridor. After these places too had been exhausted, the new ones were lying day and night in the square, uncovered, and often without any clothing at all. In principle, the pants were taken away from anyone with diarrhea who had soiled his place even once. Those who were unconscious were delirious, the dying were groaning, and the air was filled with a nauseating stench caused by diarrhea and pus, which was emitted by the uncovered, horrible phlegm and gangrene sores. The wounds of those who suffered from burns of the bones were an especially horrible sight. Such a wound turned green at first. After a few days, a black edge formed around it, and small, white-yellow worms were crawling out from the infectious sore. . . . They multiplied incredibly fast, and soon they covered the entire body of the sick man, who, at this stage of his illness, had long since lost consciousness.

Everywhere one could constantly see such pictures. Those of the sick who were still conscious tried to get up as soon as someone from the staff would walk by. With lips burned black from fever, they begged for their death. Yet it was clear to everyone that they would be "gassed."

Sometimes, it so happened that an SS man in uniform would appear on the Block. Then the dried-out hands of the sick men stretched out to him, clasped his boots, and begged with their unnaturally shining eyes for mercy killing.

"I can't take it anymore! If you believe in God—kill me!"

A kick and a laugh was the answer. After that one of the convalescent patients was ordered to clean the "soiled" boots.

The "selection" for gassing usually took place on Tuesdays. On this day, *SS-Obersturmführer* Entreß arrived from Auschwitz, and the usual inspection of the sick took place. Without any consideration for their condition of health, all of the sick were driven into the square and lined up or laid down in rows of ten. Entreß walked along the front while keeping a well-measured distance. Then he decided: Those to the right for gassing, those to the left back to the Block. Those prisoners designated for gassing remained right in the square. All others were assigned new places in the Block. During the duration of the inspection, the entire Block was cleaned because this was the only opportunity to do so. Under the supervision of Bogdans or Dr. Krause, those who were healthier and stronger rearranged the bunks, scraped off the excretions, scrubbed the walls with morning coffee, and gathered shovels full of clay, excretions from the sick with diarrhea, and trash which had piled up in the corridor. Afterwards the entire Block was sprinkled with chlorine. The door was opened so that the biting odor could escape and fresh air stream in. Then came the second "selection." This time the sick were assigned to the rooms. And because there was no chance whatsoever to save the critically ill, Dr. Schwartz therefore tried it with the lesser "cases." . . . The "better ones" were accordingly led to rooms one or two, those with typhoid fever who had a chance to recover, to room three, and the rest to room four. Most of the time, the occupants of the third and fourth rooms were already in such a condition that they could no longer take in any food. Their portions were, therefore, divided between the first two rooms. This was the only help for the lighter cases. Thanks to these divisions of the portions, every week thirty to forty men who had been threatened by death were able to leave Block number 7.

After Entreß had left the Block, the horrible work for the *Blockältesten* and the Block clerk began. Within a few hours, those prisoners who were marked for gassing were loaded onto trucks and were driven to the gas chamber. Before this time, the clerk had to single out their file cards and hand them over to the transport leader. The tattooed number of each patient had to be read off his hand. Thus, a "death report" with a fictitious cause of death had to be written down for the still-living prisoner. All of that had to be completed within about two hours. It should not be forgotten that the average number during each "selection" amounted to about 500 persons. As soon as this was done, the "preparations" for the transport began. Those of the sick who were strong enough to climb into the truck on their own were placed in the front, standing; the weaker ones were laid down in the back of the truck.

The trucks were driven to the front, the stairs were placed on the truck, and the loading began. Two men climbed into the car; the other two remained below. Those who were standing below wrote down the numbers; the others showed the sick man his place in the truck. One truck could accommodate about eighty sick people. The so-called "corpse companies" (*Leichenkommandos*) were arranged to carry those who were unconscious. These were strong, tall lads who were given special care by the camp administration. Each of them seized one sick man by the collar with one hand, seized another with the other hand, and dragged them across the floor to the stairs of the truck. In the truck, the critically ill were piled on top of each other, the weakest on the bottom and those who were still audibly groaning on top of them. The sick were loaded into the truck under the supervision of a few SS men. With their whips, they drove on those prisoners who were loading the sick. After the square was empty and the last truck was driving through the gate, the cleanup began.

Because I was, after all, healthy, I reported for work. After an hour, we scattered chlorine on the clean square, and then the "new arrivals" were expected. For several months, it continued like this on Block 7. After my return to the Block, I noticed that something very unusual was happening. The *Blockälteste* and the clerk were quarreling with each other, gesticulating with their hands, while Viktor was holding a piece of paper in his hand. During the comparison of the copied numbers with the delivered file cards, it had been discovered that a great error had occurred. The transport leader had been given a wrong card. The prisoner who had been given a "death report" was still on the Block, and Dr. Krause hoped to keep him alive. The file card for the prisoner who had been selected for gassing had, however, remained in the file.

In the general confusion which was always present during the preparation for the transport such an error could easily occur. The entire staff of the Block now deliberated what should be done in this case.

Since not even two hours had passed since the cars had departed, it was decided to go to the *Rapportführer* to clarify the entire mistake and to replace the wrong file card with the correct one. This seemed to be the simplest solution. Viktor calmed down, took the proof of the unfortunate mistake with him, and went to the gate where the orderly room of the *Blockführer* was located. However, he returned sooner than we had expected. His face was calm but his eyes moved restlessly. The *Blockführer* on duty, *SS-Rottenführer* Eckhardt, accompanied him. "Where is the 'living dead one'?" was the first question of the SS man. Someone ran to fetch him, and in the meantime, Eckhardt gave a speech:

"You are all dumb sheep heads! Presumably you have a screw loose already! You probably think that we SS men have nothing else to do than to search, erase and correct. You have become crazy! Officially, the prisoner whose file card the leader of the transport has taken with him is no longer alive. . . . His 'death report' is already in the 'orderly room'! In order to prevent further complications. . ." At that point, he discontinued because the aforementioned prisoner appeared in the door just now; he was led by an assistant attendant. He was a young Dutchman, who was rather thin, but otherwise he looked reasonably fair. He reported to Eckhardt according to protocol and stood at attention. Until now, he had not been informed of the purpose for his appearance.

"It is you? Hm... You indeed look terrific." He scrutinized him from top to bottom.

"Turn around!" The Dutchman obediently took an energetic turn.

"First class!" The voice of the *Blockführer* was clearly full of praise while his hand was already drawing his pistol. "Bend your knees a few times, and don't look around!" The prisoner's knees bounced a few times. Eckhardt moved closer and lifted up the revolver. He quickly placed the barrel of the pistol to the young man's head and fired.

"Finished! Now you don't have to change anything. The content of the report is in accordance with reality." He put his weapon into his holster and turned towards the pale Viktor. "In the future, correct such mistakes yourselves. Because of this stupid matter, I had to interrupt my skat game." He spoke the last words quite angrily. Then *Herr Rottenführer* Eckhardt strolled out of the Block.

The pallbearers undressed the dead youth and carried him below the wall.

15

AT THE BEGINNING OF the following week, we learned on Block 7 that the anticipated transport could not leave at the usual time because of the renovation of the crematory and the gas chamber. Despite that, new arrivals came uninterruptedly to the Block so that the number of the sick threatened to reach two thousand in a short time. A disastrous situation developed. Not even the smallest single place was available in order to admit the new arrivals to the Block. Even the square was overflowing with sick prisoners to such an extent that they had to be placed in layers upon layers, one on top of another.

After a brief discussion, it was decided to send Viktor to the leading physician of Birkenau, prisoner Dr. Roman Zenkteller, in order to engage his help in convincing the *Lagerältesten* to provide a second Block for the sick. This seemed to be such a simple matter that no obstacle to the realization of this plan was expected. After a while, Viktor returned. Dr. Roman Zenkteller and the *Lagerälteste* of Birkenau, the green-dot bearer, Leo Wietschorek, were accompanying him. The latter, a former criminal, had been sentenced to death in Leipzig, but a few days prior to the execution, he had been pardoned, and after the creation of Auschwitz, he was sent there. Within the camp, he had immediately been assigned a good position and disposed over life and death of the prisoners. This churl was almost two meters tall with broad shoulders, a long face, and a characteristically low forehead. Dr. Zenkteller, standing next to him, appeared almost comical. He was a little man with a stooped back, a long nose, and somewhat too long hands. These two men decided over the fate of human beings in Birkenau. Every plan of the SS found an excellent tool for its realization in each of them.

Now Viktor led these two into the square. With great efforts they wriggled through the mass of the sick lying on the ground and came to the Block. On the way, Viktor tried to justify his request by pointing to the pitiful figures lying there. Finally, they stopped at the room of the orderly of the Block.

"Yes . . . hm . . . the Block is really overcrowded," Leo determined. "But I have no other Block which I could use for this purpose. You will have to find a solution about what to do." Viktor motioned helplessly with his hand.

"But how?"

Now Dr. Zenkteller joined the discussion. "In Auschwitz, they have means to avoid overcrowding in the hospital barracks for some time now," he said meaningfully.

"I don't understand."

"You will understand it this evening. Let's go, Leo!" They turned around and left the Block. An hour later, a dispatcher came out of the orderly room of the *Blockführer* with the notice: "The *Blockführer* must come immediately to the *Rapportführer*!"

Since Viktor was absent, the clerk Piasecki went to him. After less than a quarter of an hour, he returned with a grim look on his face.

"To hell with them!" he was already cursing at the doorstep. "Do you know what that stupid ass has said?" We looked curiously at him.

"Well, we ourselves are expected to finish off the human surplus of our Block. We shall not get another Block. The new arrivals are coming continually; however, the transports have been discontinued. If it continues like that by the end of the week, we will have reached a total number of four thousand sick men. I am going crazy!"

"And what kind of advice does Zenkteller have? He ought to take care of the matter," Dr. Krause remarked naively.

Piasecki crimsoned with fury.

"Zenkteller is an even greater pig than all the other SS men put together. He made a stupid face and kept mentioning the so-called solutions of Auschwitz. I probably have to hang myself. How many dead have there been today?" he asked the silent Bogdan.

"Until now, about one hundred men."

"Insanity! Just now I received word from the *Rapportführer* that we can expect new arrivals. Yesterday they conducted another "selection" in all blocks of Auschwitz, and again they have committed three hundred people to us! Please, advise me what should be done?"

At that moment Viktor came. He inquired about the situation, reflected on it and said:

"There is only one solution. I go to Leo and turn in my *Blockaltesten* armband. I have no intention of going crazy on this Block. I am almost there already."

"We shall go together!" Piasecki decided.

And without another word, they left the Block. Bogdan spoke a few more words with Dr. Krause, tore the cap off his head, and threw it to the ground saying, "I shall go with them! I am not even thinking about remaining alone in this hell."

All three men returned much sooner than expected. Viktor, very troubled, sank down at the table and covered his face with his hands. Bogdan busied himself with the files and Piasecki cursed for the second time already when he reached the doorway.

"Beasts! Damned pigs! I would like to get these dogs into my hands. I would cut them to pieces with a razor, then I would salt them, and after that I would roast them slowly over an open fire!"

"Well then, is anything new happening?" Dr. Krause asked.

"Something new? Nothing special! All three of us were told that a concentration camp is not an institution where one can leave his post . . . he who will not follow orders will be considered a traitor, and there are bullets ready for traitors . . . to put it plainly, we received the order to select one hundred sick men for injections. In the evening some kind of pig will come and conduct the 'operation' that should prevent overcrowding!"

"That is simply horrible!"

Suddenly, Viktor got up. "I'll go and work on the lice control." He turned to Piasecki. "You will make sure that the men for injection are chosen by six o'clock." He nodded his head and departed quickly from the Block.

For a while there was silence. Then Piasecki erupted. "Did you hear the *Herr Blockältesten*? Just now he remembered the lice control, and I am supposed to select the people for their death. Fortunately, I am not stupider than Viktor. I just remembered that the *Blockälteste* from Block 4 had asked me to make compresses on his Block. . . ." He got up and took the first-aid box, which was hanging on the wall. "Look, I am leaving, and you, Bogdan, make sure that everything will be in order."

"Lightning shall strike you!" Glinski interrupted him. "I am also going to find a reason to leave the Block. Don't even think that I am dumber than you are. Furthermore, Dr. Krause will be here. It will be much easier for him to carry out the selection than it is for me. After all, he is a physician."

Dr. Krause turned pale. "I'm begging you, don't leave me alone. I am a physician. I am supposed to help and heal, and not kill. . . . And furthermore, I am a Jew! If you don't carry out an order, you will still get off lightly. But I will be killed immediately. Please, show some mercy."

The old doctor's voice was trembling. Tears came to his eyes. Piasecki stayed. For a while he looked at the shaking physician, and then he threw the first-aid box onto the table.

"I must say that we are all pigs. Krause is right. I am not going to leave the Block."

"Then I am staying too!" decided Bogdan.

During the next few minutes, we discussed the situation, trying to find a satisfactory solution. Kracz, one of the prisoners who had been silent until now, participated in our discussion. He had previously been a leader of a Polish Riding Brigade. After a stay of six weeks in a Bunker, the local Gestapo had transferred him to the Punishment Company (SK). From there he was later brought to Block 7.

"Please excuse me when I enter the conversation about a matter which is only of concern to the staff of the Block. I too am slowly losing my wits. What is really your concern? To save the lives of one hundred sick people? No! Under no circumstances will you be able to save them. For you, the problem is that you do not want to bring about the death of these human beings. Yes or no?"

A general nodding of heads was the answer.

"If you, therefore, do not want to choose the death candidates, if you do not have the courage to participate in the death of other prisoners, then you ought to at least have the courage to state that clearly. You obviously do not want to participate in this act, and I do not know of any power which could force you to do that. In the worst of scenarios, you will lose your life but at least as human beings and not as malicious murderers, even in a forced way. That certainly is obvious. . . ."

The silence which entered after these words lasted for quite some time. It was a heavy burden on all of us. Finally Piasecki spoke.

"You are right, Janek. What you have said is indeed very clear. I should have immediately thought of that. It is quite obvious that in the camp I have almost forgotten how to think clearly. I thank you!" He gave Janek his hand, which the other squeezed tightly.

The two hours which we still had at our disposal until six o'clock we spend in general conversation. During that time no word fell about the topic in question. A few minutes before six o'clock, Dr. Zenkteller came to the Block.

"Well, is everything ready?"

Piasecki shook his head.

"No!"

"Why is that? You should have selected one hundred persons for injections."

Piasecki continued to busy himself with the file cards. "What do you mean by 'you'?"

"Well, you who are here on the Block."

"No, Doctor, we are not going to select anyone!"

Zenkteller looked at him with surprise.

"What does that mean? Uprising?"

"No uprising!" Piasecki responded calmly without raising his head from the card file. "There is really no one on this Block who would be qualified to conduct an objective selection. I am informed about the files, the reports, and the announcements. The *Blockälteste* has his work in the camp, the staff of the medical attendants is not at all qualified, and the only physician became ill two days ago. . . . Furthermore, we do not follow the customs of Auschwitz, even though you really like them. In Auschwitz, however, the selections are a matter for the SS men, and not for the prisoners."

"Of course, I understand. You gentlemen have too soft a nature, haven't you? I shall not refrain from reporting this incident to the *Lagerführer*. In the meantime, I request that you prepare the sick for inspection. I shall personally conduct the selection."

"As you wish."

At 6:30 p.m. one hundred naked prisoners were standing in room number 4. Dr. Zenkteller had marked them for death.

Everyone was expecting, with horror, the arrival of "Professor" Klehr, who was to administer the lethal injections. Around seven o'clock, a dispatcher came with the message that Klehr would not come. After a brief reflection, Dr. Zenkteller ran quickly to the *Rapportführer*. After a quarter of an hour, he returned. Under his arm he was carrying a sterilizer, and in his hand he had a bottle filled with grey liquid.

"I have spoken with the *Rapportführer*. I myself shall give the injections. However, since I have no Phenol, I will use Lysol. Let us hope that everything will go all right. I need four men to assist me."

Without saying a word, Piasecki assigned four assistant medical attendants. It turned out much worse than Dr. Zenkteller had anticipated. Lysol was good for the killing of insects, but it turned out to be too weak for the elimination of human beings. The injected five-centimeter dose was not close to sufficient. The sick who had received the injections began to scream inhumanly. In horrible pain, they fell to the ground. A foam of blood gushed from their mouths.

An utter chaos developed during which time Dr. Zenkteller completely lost his head. With a full syringe, he ran from one prisoner to another in order to supplement the dose. The rest of the death candidates ran in all directions with horrifying screams. In room number 4, only about fifteen half-dead human beings remained, including Dr. Zenkteller, who, soiled with blood, looked monstrous. He was continually scolding his helpers. After a while, however, his screams and the groaning of the dying fell silent. It was obvious that he could not continue his "work." By the way, even Dr. Zenkteller appeared to be fed up. Before he left the Block, he even said to Piasecki:

"It was not as simple as it seemed to me . . . ".

No one, however, answered him. He wiped his hands with a towel and said, while still standing in the door:

"I am going to Leo. We have to think of something else."

On the following day, we learned what this "something else" was. Early in the morning, the *Lagerführer* Leo and Dr. Zenkteller appeared, accompanied by a *Sonderkommando* which consisted of twenty prisoners. At the head of this command, there stood the infamous murderer of the camp, Götzel.

"These men," *SS-Hauptscharführer* Fitze explained to the *Blockältesten*, "remain on Block 7. They do not belong to the staff and are only under my personal command. All of you, *Blockältester*, representatives, and medical attendants have nothing to say. These twenty men shall receive triple rations of food. Is this understood?"

"Yes, Sir!"

That afternoon, Götzel's *Arbeitskommando* began to work. Half of the rooms were covered with blankets, and all the sick were transferred to other rooms.

Then Götzel, accompanied by four stocky lads under his command, went to the square. He walked by the individual sick men and pointed at them. The next moment, they were led into the separated section of room number 4. There they were received by the other men of the command. A short procedure followed: A blow with a club to the neck of the sick man, which made him unconscious. Thereupon, one man of the command pressed his foot on the throat of the one lying on the floor until death set in. . . .

Thus, the problem of overcrowding in Block 7 was solved. Götzel's daily "work quota" fluctuated between 150 and 200 sick people. . . .

16

Symek Rosenthal was a small craftsman from Cichenau. The conditions of the War had driven him from one place to another, thrown him from one ghetto to the next. Finally he "landed" in Birkenau with a large transport of members of his religious community. The rest of his family: his father, his brother, and his wife, shared his fate.

The entire transport was immediately divided after they had reached the train station of Auschwitz. Symek now had to march on foot to the camp without the other members of his family. An SS officer explained that the other part of the transport would be taken by car to the camp. In the camp, a number was tattooed onto Symek's left hand, everything he owned had been taken away, his head was shaven bald, and he was "deloused." His camp clothing now consisted only of torn rags. He had to sew a six-pointed star onto the chest of his clothes, and he also had to sew the number which had been tattooed on his hand onto a small piece of cloth. After this was done, a lanky SS man began to beat the new arrivals. He did not care whom or where his heavy club was hitting. Symek Rosenthal had seen a lot during the last three years: In the ghetto, corpses of people whom hunger or the SS men's bullets had killed, or Jewish work companies, who were butchered to pieces. And yet in the ghetto everything had looked different than here in the camp. In the ghetto he had still been lucky. He had not been beaten that often because he had always been able to flee and to hide somewhere. The ghetto had, after all, closed residential districts which were at his disposal, where other people were still living, and where one could feel at home. Was it therefore surprising that Symek Rosenthal, despite everything, was not afraid in the ghetto? But here, everything was different. The barrack was dark and locked. The lanky SS man worked him over with his club, and it was not possible to escape from these four walls. Therefore, it was only now that Symek Rosenthal began to grasp his situation. It is true that over there in the ghetto one was surrounded by walls, yet one was nevertheless free. Here in the camp, there were only violent SS men and mistreated prisoners. Symek Rosenthal, for the first time in his life, fell into despair, and for the first time, he experienced a sense of fear.

After about an hour of aimless beating, the SS man was getting tired. Here and there, massacred human beings were lying around. The SS man looked at the others and ordered them to line up. Gasping, he asked whether everyone now realized what it was like in a concentration camp. "Yes, Sir!" they all answered. Indeed, now everyone was informed about exactly what he could expect in the camp. The SS man walked up and down the front and chose about thirty prisoners, among whom was Symek Rosenthal. They had to line up in rows of three and march with him to Block 3. This Block was, like the SK and Block 7, separated from the rest of the camp by a wall. In the square, the SS man makes a stop. In an almost fatherly tone, he explains to the prisoners that they did need not be afraid and that it would go well with them in the camp. Although they would be used for unpleasant work, through this work they would certainly survive the camp. If, however, anyone should not like the work, he could report to him.

The *Blockälteste* of Block 3 was also wearing a star on his chest. He recorded everything according to protocol, and now they were allowed to go to their barrack rooms. Even their nightmare, the SS man, suddenly disappeared, after he had announced that he would arrive at four o'clock the next morning.

The new arrivals noticed immediately that they had taken the places of strangers in their rooms. On the bunks there were still blankets, clothing, and, above all, food in such amounts as they had not seen for a long time. The *Blockälteste* remarked that everything they would find, they could consider their own property. That seemed somewhat strange; however, no one gave it much thought for a long time. They rushed to the food because they had had nothing to eat for several days. White bread, butter, lard, delicious sausages, honey, sugar, all these wonderful delicacies were plentiful and at hand. During the next hour, no one spoke a word. Everyone was eating in silence and thought about nothing else. And then someone went to the *Blockältesten* to ask if he could put on the clothes which had been left there. The *Blockälteste* allowed it.

Then the clothes were put on, and the numbers and stars were sewn on. Symek Rosenthal was the first to finish it. He gathered a few heavy, wool blankets and lay down. Everything was incomprehensible to him. After all, he was not taken to the camp in order to fill himself with white bread and butter. . . . Something was not right here. The clothing which was found scattered on the ground could not have come from the camp. In fact, in the entire stockroom, there was not a single piece of white bread, not a gram of butter, not to speak of the wonderful sausages from the civilian sector.

Without a doubt, however, he had found these things in his bunk. From whence did they come? Who had delivered them here? Where was this human being now?

At the moment when they stepped into the Block, there was no one to be seen. And yet traces of their occupants were found in every bunk. With such reflections, Symek Rosenthal fell asleep.

Early in the morning, he was awakened by noise, and no sooner had he come to his senses than someone grabbed him by the foot and dragged him out of his bunk. In the semidarkness he recognized the well-known figure of the lanky SS man from yesterday. Within five minutes, the thirty men were ready for the roll call. They were counted, and then they marched on.

The camp was still empty. They marched through the gate through which they had entered the camp yesterday. Soon they found themselves on a muddy road. After a few kilometers, they arrived at a small birch forest. Here a sign forbade, under penalty of death, entrance into the small forest. Even the SS man needed to have a special pass. Soon they saw a few little houses, which were surrounded by barbed wire. Around the barbed wire stood SS guards, armed with pistols. Symek Rosenthal began to be afraid. Instinctively, he felt that he stood in front of the unveiling of a gruesome mystery.

The tall SS man ordered them to halt in front of one of the little houses. Obediently, everyone stopped. The SS man drew his pistol and said that they had already arrived at the right place. They would soon begin their work, and if anyone should not like it, he could report to him! While saying this, he pointed significantly to his pistol. After that, the entire column was divided into groups of ten men each. The SS man appointed a *Vorarbeiter* for each group, whom he held responsible for the accuracy and efficiency of the work. Symek was assigned to the group which had to work in the house in front of which they were now standing.

From the outside, this little house looked somewhat odd. Instead of the usual windows, it had large shutters which looked like a window screen and could be locked with iron screws. On the place where the shutters were to tighten the openings, they were fit with rubber which guaranteed an exact insulation.

On the command "Get to work!" the prisoners, led by an SS man, went into the little house. It was divided into three parts. To the left there was a door with the inscription "Waiting Room." To the right there was a board on which "Bathroom" was inscribed in three languages.

Symek and his group entered the waiting room first. A number of suitcases were scattered on the floor; the benches and coat hooks were filled with pieces of clothing and underwear. The SS man ordered the men to carry all that into a barn which was located behind the little house. He kicked someone in the lower abdomen to reinforce his order. With a jump, Symek landed in the opposite corner of the waiting room. He was about to grab the first suitcase when he saw a comrade, who walked by him, carrying in his hand a heap of suits and jackets among which he noticed a strangely familiar men's jacket.

He threw the suitcase to the ground and stopped the one who was walking by. Nervously he pulled the jacket out of the large bundle and held it to the light. He saw clearly how it turned black before his eyes, and he had to gasp for breath. Last night, this jacket had still been worn by his father. He swallowed his suddenly thickened saliva and felt, with a trembling hand, into the pocket of the jacket. The old, brown money purse came to light. It was worn out from yearlong use. He was so familiar with it because his father had taken money out of it more than once to buy him some sweets or to pay larger amounts for him in later years. Motionlessly and as if in a daze, he stood there for some time without understanding how his father's jacket could have landed here.

And where is his father now?

A blow and the screeching voice of the SS man brought him to his senses. He broke down, threw away the jacket, and ran with the next two suitcases out of the door . . .

"Where is my father, where?!"

During the next minutes, he could think only about this. Uninterruptedly, he ran into the waiting room and carried out heavy suitcases. This question, however, did not give him peace. The stooped, grey figure of his father stood continually before his eyes, and his voice sounded in his ears.

Where is he? . . .

In the meantime, the waiting room had become empty. The working prisoners went to the barn. On orders of the SS man, they had to sort the suits, coats, underwear, and shoes. They also had to empty the pockets and open the suitcases. They had to throw the entire content of it into a certain box: food into one which was marked as "food"; the soap, toothpaste, cologne, etc. into another one, and medications into the third box. Gold, money and other valuables which were found, they had to bring to the SS man, who was sitting in front of a rather small box.

Symek began to pick out the belongings of his father. He found almost all of them.

Suddenly, there was a terrible outcry from a prisoner. Screaming, he fell unconscious to the ground. A great confusion followed. The SS man poured a bucket of water on the head of the prisoner, who soon regained his consciousness. When he got up, the SS man asked him what had happened. The still half-unconscious prisoner burst out, "Those are the things of my boy. Where is he? What have you done to him?"

The SS man started laughing, drew his pistol, and fired a shot. He did that as calmly as if he were lighting a cigarette. The prisoner fell silent. He sank to the ground, bleeding profusely. His body convulsed a few times, he opened his mouth and his eyes wide, and then he lay there motionlessly. The SS man put his weapon away and said in his usual tone, as if this incident had not occurred, "Throw him into the square!"

From this moment onward, Symek Rosenthal no longer thought about where his father might be. Without thinking, he emptied one suitcase after another and mechanically distributed the contents into the different boxes. After this work was completed, the SS man gave orders to line up. He counted the group and began the bodily inspection.

Now they returned to the little house. The SS man halted in front of the door marked "bathroom."

"Carry out all the corpses!"

Henceforth no one had any questions any longer, and no one was surprised when the door was opened. The bare walls were painted white. The stony floor was covered with a wooden grid as is customary in a swimming pool. On the ceiling there were short pipes which had showers. And on the floor: Corpses. They were naked, terribly cramped, piled one on top of another. Out of their dead, glassy eyes, stared horror and pain. . . .

The SS man drew attention to himself again. He beat someone and began to yell.

With their trembling hands, they took the cold bodies and carried them outside. Symek Rosenthal already carried the fifth body into the square. Each time he entered the "bathroom," he looked around with dull eyes. Finally, the last time, he found what he had been seeking: His father! He was lying on the floor, covered with other bodies. He had a tinge of blue lush but looked somewhat different from the rest of the dead. His long, grey beard covered his breast; he had closed his eyes. He could not think a thought and moved as if hypnotized. He pulled his father to his chest and held him tightly with both arms. He began to walk continuously, slowly, as if at a funeral. When he arrived at the heap of corpses which was piled up in front of the little house, he stood there for a while and searched for a good place. Then he placed him to the side of the entire heap so that they could not pile another one on his father. Gently, he laid down the corpse, looked at him with deference for a moment, and returned to his work.

That evening, the secret of the food and pieces of clothing which were found in number 3 was disclosed. They belonged to the previous *Sonderkommando*, consisting of 180 men, which was loaded into cars one day and driven to Auschwitz. There they had all been shot in the square of the crematory.

From this day onward, Symek Rosenthal became a different person. He seldom spoke a word and never smiled. Instead he worked with a strange self-denial. In addition, when he returned to the Block, he immediately went to bed. He was therefore designated as an exemplary worker of the "*Sonderkommando*."

One day, Symek became ill with typhoid fever, which meant he was admitted to us on Block 7. At that time, there came a special order from the *Kommandoführer* that Symek Rosenthal should not be presented for the "gassing inspection." It did not take very long before his strong constitution overcame the illness and Symek's health condition improved steadily. I became better acquainted with him. After only about two weeks, I learned about those events, his own "Passion Story," as narrated by himself. From these days onward, we talked more often.

17

In mid-July, Viktor called for me.

"I have bad news for you," he started immediately, when I had hardly sat down. "As of August 1, you will have to return to the SK. There has been a change which will make it impossible for healthy prisoners to remain in this Block," he added apologetically.

"If it has to be," I said briefly. Viktor looked at me steadily.

"How long have you actually been in the SK?"

"Fifteen months."

He scratched his head.

"Good heavens! Hm . . ." Suddenly, he looked sharply at me, as if he had an idea.

"Have you already reported to the rapport?"

"To what kind of a rapport? Last year I had to appear before a punishment rapport. At that time, however, I was sentenced to the SK."

"Were you given a specific time frame for the punishment?"

I shook my head.

"No."

"If I were you, I would go to the *Lagerführer* with the request that he inform you about the maximum penalty. That is certainly no risk. In the worst-case scenario, you would get one at your teeth for your audacity."

I thought about it briefly. It was certainly not a bad idea. Nothing worse than a longer stay in the SK could happen to me.

"How does one go about that?"

"It is very simple . . . I take you to the *Rapportbuch* this evening. Theoretically, every prisoner certainly has the right to personally petition the *Lagerführer* if he thinks that an injustice has been done to him. . . ." Viktor laughed. "Of course, I have never heard that anyone had come that far.

Usually he disappeared already on his way. In spite of that fact, many foreigners who visited the camp saw the *Rapportbuch* and were full of praise regarding the justice of our supervisors. Hm . . . You are still on my Block, and therefore you can circumvent certain channels. You do not need to be afraid of the *Blockältesten* and *Blockführer*. And I will speak with the *Rapportführer* so that he will allow you to proceed. . . . In fact, I am giving him his daily compresses just now. Well, then?"

"Bring me the *Rapportbuch*!" I decided.

In the evening, I wrote on a piece of paper that prisoner 8214 requested to speak in person with the *Lagerführer* regarding a matter concerning the camp. Viktor confirmed it and added that only the *Lagerführer* personally could deal with this matter.

In the morning the *Rapportbuch* went to Auschwitz. I passed the following day with nervous anticipation. Will my request be accepted or denied?

It was accepted! One day, a piece of paper came from the orderly room informing me that I had to be prepared to march at ten o'clock and wait at the gate. The best wishes of my comrades accompanied me as I marched along the Auschwitz Street an hour later. In the camp, I was assigned a clerk from the orderly room, named Kurt Makula. Together with him, I went to the work room of the *Lagerführer*.

In front of the door, however, I had to stop. I was so irritated and nervous that I was couldn't even bring a normal sound out of my throat. Something tightened my throat, my knees were shaking, and my hands were trembling. . . .

Kurt seemed to understand my condition because he did not say a word. He only tapped me on the shoulder. Finally, I was calm. I repeated the report formula and knocked at the door.

A brief "Come in!" was the answer.

I opened the door, let Kurt go ahead of me, and finally I myself entered. As tight as a violin string, I stood at attention and gave my report as loudly as possible, bearing in mind that such a bellowing was the only way to force the attention of the so-called "official places."

"Prisoner 8214 is reporting obediently with the request . . ."

Aumeier, whom I knew quite well from the blood bath of the "red-dot bearers," looked curiously at me.

"Well, what do you want?"

I pulled myself together again and yelled so that the windows rumbled:

"Fifteen months ago, I was sentenced by *SS–Hauptsturmführer* Fritzsch to twenty-five blows with a cane and to the Punishment Company (SK). During the entire time of my stay, I have not committed a new offence. Therefore, I request that a date be set for the completion of the punishment. . . ."

Aumeier looked at me as if I were a marvelous thing.

"What? You have spent fifteen months in the SK? That is impossible. How did you do that?" he said with real surprise.

"I worked industriously!" I yelled again.

He nodded his head.

"I really should send you to an exhibition. You are a rarity in the camp."

"There are other extremely rare ones," I quickly threw into the conversation.

"Really? There are still others who are in the SK even longer than you?"

"I know three men: Gibs, Pilecki, and Röhmer."

"Hm . . . hm . . ." He wrote down the three names and then said, "Well, you may remove your black dot. I discharge you from the SK. However, I am doing so only because you have behaved well, understood?" he quickly added.

"Yes, Sir!"

"Be off!"

I clicked my heels. "Prisoner 8214 is asking to leave. . . ."

When I got to the street of the Camp, the sun was shining brighter than ever before. . . .

Literature[1]

Adler, H.G., Langbein, H., Lingens-Rainer, E. *Auschwitz: Zeugnisse und Berichte.* Frankfurt, 1988.

Broszat, M. (Hg). *Rudolf Höß–Kommandant in Auschwitz.* München, 1988.

Czech, Dauta. *Kalendarium der Ereignisse vom Konzentrationslager Auschwitz-Birkenau* 1939-1945. München, 1989.

Hieberg, Raul. *Die Vernichtung der europäischen Juden.* 3 Bände. Frankfurt, 1990.

Kautsky, Benedikt. *Teufel und Verdammte.* Zürich, 1945.

Klee, E., Dressen, W., Reiss, V. *"Schöne Zeiten," —Judenmord aus der Sicht der Täter und Gaffer.* Frankfurt, 1989.

Kogon, Eugen. *Der SS-Staat.* München, 1974.

Langbein, Hermann. *Die Stärkeren.* Köln, 1982.

Langbein, Hermann. *Menschen in Auschwitz.* Wien, 1987.

Langbein, Hermann. *Nicht wie die Schafe zur Schlachtbank. Widerstand in den Nationalsozialistischen Konzentrationslagern.* Frankfurt, 1980.

Levi, Primo. *Ist das ein Mensch? Die Atempause.* München, 1990.

Levi, Primo. *Die Untergegangenen und die Geretteten.* München, 1990.

Mitscherlich, Alexander, Mitscherlich, Margarete. *Die Unfähigkeit zu Trauern.* München, 1977.

Steger, Bernd, Tiele, Günter. *Der dunkle Schatten—Leben mit Auschwitz.* Marburg, 1980.

1.. Translator's note: I have retained the original format of the bibliography to ensure the accuracy of the cited editions.

Editorial Remarks[1]

THE NAMES OF THE people cited in this book were corrected where they were incorrect in the 1948 edition. However, it is possible that the correct spelling of further names may differ slightly from those published here.

The following is known about the fate of the SS criminals whom Rozanski cited:

Aumeier, Hans.
SS–Hauptsturmführer (Schutzhaftlagerführer)
Born 1906. Death Penalty (Poland). Executed 1947.

Entreß, Dr. Friederich.
SS–Hauptsturmführer (SS Physician)
Born 1914. Death Penalty (USA). Executed 1946.

Fritzsch, Karl.
SS–Hauptsturmführer (Schutzhaftlagerführer)
Born 1903. Died 1945.

Klehr, Josef.
SS–Oberscharführer (Sanitatsdienstgrad)
Born 1904. During the Auschwitz Trial in 1965, sentenced to life in prison because of 475 murder cases. Died 1988.

1. Translator's note: This is a list of important information about the SS criminals. Therefore, I have retained the original wording for the sake of accuracy. The various ranks can be found in glossaries A and B on the next two pages.

Moll, Otto.
SS-Hauptscharführer (Blockführer)
Born 1915. Death Penalty (USA). Executed 1946.

Palitzsch, Gerhard.
SS-Hauptscharführer (Rapportführer in Auschwitz, later Auschwitz I).
Born 1913. He fell into disgrace and was arraigned before an SS Court. He fell in Hungary, 1944.

Schillinger, Josef.
SS-Hauptscharführer (Rapportführer in Birkenau)
In 1943, he was killed in the Concentration Camp [KZ] Bergen-Belsen by a Jewish woman while she was being admitted there.

Schwarz, Heinrich.
SS-Hauptsturmführer (Arbeitseinsatzführer, later commandant in Monowitz, Auschwitz III) Born 1906. Death Penalty (France). Ex ecuted 1947.

Translator's Appendix A

General Comparative List of SS and Military Ranks[1] (Listed according to ranks)

Reichsführer-SS: General of the Army
SS-Oberstgruppenführer: General
SS-Obergruppenführer: Lieutenant General
SS-Gruppenführer: Major General
SS-Brigadeführer: Brigadier General
SS-Oberführer: No equivalent
SS-Standartenführer: Colonel
SS-Obersturmbannführer: Major
SS-Hauptsturmführer: Captain
SS-Obersturmführer: 1st Lieutenant
SS-Untersturmführer: 2nd Lieutenant
SS-Sturmscharführer: Master Sergeant
SS-Hauptscharführer: Technical Sergeant
SS-Oberscharführer: Staff Sergeant
SS-Unterscharführer: Corporal
SS-Rottenführer: Private First Class
SS-Sturmmann: Private
SS-Mann: No equivalent

1. Eugene Kogon et al., *Nazi Mass Murder: A Documentary History of the Use of Poison Gas* (New Haven: Yale University Press, 1993), 227.